たのしく読める

日本のくらし12か月

Moons, Months and Seasons

A Pre-intermediate Japanese Reader

国際日本語研究所編

杏文堂

目
CONTENTS
次

はじめに

　「日本のくらし12か月―Moons, Months and Seasons」は400時間程度初級レベルの学習が終わった日本語学習者を対象とした読み教材です。

　近年、日本語学習者の多様化にともなって、さまざまな学習教材が必要とされていますが、本書はとくに初級終了レベルの学習者が、気軽に、簡単に読むことができ、日本人の生活を知ることができる「読みもの」をめざして作られました。そのため教室で教師の指導のもとに使うこともできますし、ひとりで勉強したい場合にも十分使えるように工夫されています。教室で使う場合も文法構造を学ぶためのテキストとしてではなく、これまでに学習した日本語の知識をもとに、日本人の生活を知るための「読みもの」として使っていただきたいと思います。

　本書は次のような特色があります。
1．日本人の1年の生活を12か月に分け、各月ごとに新聞や日常会話でよく見聞きするトピックと語彙をとりあげています。
2．各月の本文は800字前後にまとめられ、初級文法を終わった学習者が無理なく読み進めるような文で書かれています。ただし、日本人がよく使うことばや日本人の話題について理解できるように、語彙については日本人の成人のことばとして日常のものを使っています。
3．本文は漢字かなまじり文で書かれていますが、読みやすさを考慮して、もっとも基本的なもの以外の漢字は全部「漢字の読みかた」のページにふりがなとともに載せてあります。
4．本文で取りあげたトピックや語彙の中でとくに日本の文化や歴史、風土にかかわっているものについては、イラストや写真を載せ、英語でわかりやすく説明してあります。
5．また、それとともに、本文中のことばや表現で初級終了レベルの学習者にはやや難しいと思われるものは、巻末の語彙リストに英訳を記してあります。
6．さらに本文の理解をたすけるために、各月ごとに英文が付けてあります。

　以上のような特徴を持った本書の使い方はいろいろあるでしょう。1月から読み始めて12月まで読んでいっても良いですし、自分の読みたい月から読むこ

ともできます。イラストや写真のページの英語の解説を読んで、日本人の1年のくらしについて知るというのも、本書の利用法のひとつでしょう。もちろん、本文を読み、漢字を勉強し、ひとつひとつのことばや表現の意味や用法を学習するという使い方もあると思います。

　また、本書は英語を媒介語（ばいかいご）として日本語を教える日本語教師にも役に立つでしょう。日本文化や四季の行事などを、イラストや写真とともにわかりやすく、ていねいな英語で説明してありますから、外国人に日本文化を紹介するときにも有効に活用できます。

　本書が日本語学習者の日本語の上達と日本理解に役立てば幸いです。

　　　　1992年2月

　　　　　　　　　　　　　　　　　　　　国際日本語研究所

Preface

"Nihon no Kurashi Jūnikagetsu — **Moons, Months and Seasons"** is reading material for students studying the Japanese language. It is written mainly for the pre-intermediate students who have finished a beginner's course of about 400 hours.

Since the number of those who study the Japanese language has increased, there is need for a greater variety of study materials today. This book is meant for pre-intermediate students to enjoy reading without much difficulty, learning, at the same time, about everyday life in Japan. It is designed to be used both as a textbook in the classroom under a teacher's guidance and as reading material to be enjoyed by students on their own. We recommend it be used not as a text to study sentence structures but as reading material to come to know Japanese customs — the background of the language.

This book has the following features:

1. Japanese everyday life is depicted month by month in 12 chapters, and each chapter deals with the subjects and vocabulary that are often encountered in the mass media and daily life.

2. A text of approximately 800 characters for each month is written mostly in simple sentences for pre-intermediate students to understand easily with their knowledge of basic grammar. Yet, the vocabulary, intentionally drawn from words in use among average Japanese adults today, might help the students to follow everyday conversations in town.

3. This book is written in *kanji* and *kana*, and for easier reading all *kanji* except the most fundamental ones are listed, with their readings, on the "How to Read *Kanji*" pages.

4. Illustrations and photographs with English captions are provided for better understanding of subjects and vocabulary that have deep roots in Japanese culture, customs or history.

5. At the end of this book, there is a list of vocabulary and phrases difficult for pre-intermediate students. They are accompanied by English equivalents and explanations.

6. For reference, at the end of each chapter an English version of the main text is available.

With the features above, this book can be used in various ways. You may start reading from January through December, or just pick any month you like. You might perhaps read just the English text and the captions of the illustrations and photographs to find out about Japanese life in months and seasons. Needless to say, you may also read the text to study *kanji* and learn the meaning and usage of each word.

This book will surely be useful for teachers who teach the Japanese language in English. Japanese cultural and seasonal events and activities explained in English with illustrations and photographs might show Japanese people, also, ways to introduce Japanese culture to foreigners. It could be highly recommended for students and families planning to live overseas.

It is nothing but our pleasure if *"Nihon no Kurashi J̄unikagetu*—Moons, **Months and Seasons"** could help diligent students of the Japanese language all over the world, planting in their hearts the seeds of interest both in the language and in the culture, leading toward greater progress in their studies.

February, 1992

KIRJSI.

1月
JANUARY

睦月（むつき）

1日　元日（がんじつ）
4日　御用始め（ごようはじ）
7日　七草がゆ（ななくさ）
15日　成人の日（せいじん）（ひ）
22日ごろ　大寒（だいかん）

　1月1日は「元日（がんじつ）」といいますが、この日は日本人にとって1年の始まりを表す大切な日です。

　正月には、玄関や門に正月かざりをします。昔は門松、しめかざりなどをしましたが、今ではドアー用の輪かざりなど簡単なものもあります。

5　元日の朝を「元旦（がんたん）」といって、元旦には家族そろっておとそを飲み、おぞうに、おせち料理を食べて新年を祝います。子供たちは両親からお年玉をもらいます。多くの人々は1年の幸せを願って神社や寺院に初詣（はつもうで）に行きます。これらは正月の伝統的な行事ですが、最近ではホテルや温泉地、スキー場、海外で正月をすごす人も多くなりました。

10　元日には年賀状がまとめて配達されます。年賀状には新年のあいさつといっしょにその年のえとや家族の写真を印刷したものが多くあります。それを見るのも正月の楽しみの一つです。

　また元日、2日、3日の「正月三が日」は銀行、役所、ほとんどの会社、商店が休みになります。この休みに親類や知人、会社の上司などの家に年始回り

15　をしたりします。

　4日は官公庁の御用始めです。会社も、このころから年末年始の休暇を終えて、仕事始めとなるところが多くなります。

　7日には七草がゆを食べる習慣が古くからあります。七草がゆは春の七草を入れたおかゆです。これを食べると1年中健康ですごせると伝えられています。

20　15日は「成人の日」です。二十歳（はたち）になった人を祝い、成人式を行います。

　中旬には大相撲初場所が東京の両国国技館であり、15日間の熱戦で優勝者が決まります。

　21日ごろが「大寒（だいかん）」です。松の内のはなやいだ気分も終わって、寒さがさらにきびしくなります。

漢字のよみかた

ついたち 1日	がんじつ 元日	はじ 始まり	あらわ 表す	たいせつ 大切な	げんかん 玄関
むかし 昔	かどまつ 門松	わ 輪かざり	かんたん 簡単な	5 がんたん 元旦	かぞく 家族
いわ 祝います	こども 子供たち	りょうしん 両親	としだま お年玉	しあわ 幸せ	ねが 願って
じんじゃ 神社	じいん 寺院	はつもうで 初詣	でんとうてき 伝統的な	ぎょうじ 行事	さいきん 最近
おんせんち 温泉地	じょう スキー場	かいがい 海外	10 ねんがじょう 年賀状	はいたつ 配達されます	しゃしん 写真
いんさつ 印刷した	たの 楽しみ	ひと 一つ	ふつか 2日	みっか 3日	しょうがつさん にち 正月三が日
やくしょ 役所	しょうてん 商店	しんるい 親類	ちじん 知人	じょうし 上司	ねんしまわ 年始回り
15 よっか 4日	かんこうちょう 官公庁	ごようはじ 御用始め	ねんまつねんし 年末年始	きゅうか 休暇	お 終えて
しごとはじ 仕事始め	なのか 7日	ななくさ 七草がゆ	しゅうかん 習慣	い 入れた	いちねんじゅう 1年中
けんこう 健康	つた 伝えられて	20 せいじん ひ 成人の日	はたち 二十歳	せいじんしき 成人式	おこな 行います
ちゅうじゅん 中旬	おおずもうはつばしょ 大相撲初場所	りょうごくこくぎかん 両国国技館	ねっせん 熱戦	ゆうしょうしゃ 優勝者	き 決まります
だいかん 大寒	まつ うち 松の内	きぶん 気分	お 終わって	さむ 寒さ	

9

Osechi Ryōri　おせち料理

Osechi ryōri originally meant dishes served on seasonal festive occasions as an offering to the gods.

New Year's Day has been considered as one of the most important festive events. A variety of ingredients is prepared and arranged artistically in a set of layered lacquer-boxes; such as seasoned herring roe, sweet black beans, seaweed-rolls, sliced strings of carrot-radish salad, cooked rootvegetables and so on. Nowadays Chinese and Western dishes are added, and ready-made *osechi*-sets are available at any department store. *Osechi* dishes are made ahead as preserved food and served through the first three days of the year, so women of the family can take a break from daily cooking during the New Year holiday period.

O-toso　おとそ

O-toso is spiced *sake* with medicinal herbs and served in a decorative lacquered *sake* pot and cups to celebrate New Year's Day. It aids digestion and is effective for a stomach heavy with New Year's dishes. *O-toso* spices are sold in tea-bag style to be steeped in *sake*. It is said to drive away evil and preserve health.

Shimekazari　しめかざり

O-zōni　おぞうに

O-zōni is a special dish for the New Year. It contains rice cakes (*mochi*) in plain broth with little fish, or chicken and vegetables such as trefoil leaves, mushrooms and bamboo shoots.

In the Kanto district, plain soup is served with square rice cakes. In the Kansai district, *miso* soup is served with round rice cakes.

The way of cooking *o-zōni* varies among regions or families, and each district boasts its own specialty.

Shimekazari is a decorative, sacred straw rope festooned with strips of white paper. It is decorated with a piece of bitter orange, a lobster, and green fern leaves. It is hung above the entrance of a house to purify the

Kadomatsu　門　松

A New Year's decoration is for inviting the god of the year and for welcoming ancestral spirits. It is set up with the hope for longevity, prosperity and constancy, on either or both sides of the front entrance of the house. It is composed of pine boughs, bamboo stalks and plum-tree sprigs, and it is regarded as the residence of the god of the year. There are also simple ones that are made of pine branches wrapped with Japanese paper.

home for the New Year. Bitter orange is symbolic of continued good health in the family, and lobster is a symbol of longevity.

A house with *shimekazari* is believed to be pure, with no devils able to enter.

Otoshidama お年玉

Otoshidama is a monetary gift presented to children at the New Year.

The amount of money varies with the age of children and family circumstances. Average total amount of monetary gifts for elementary and secondary school children is about 30,000 yen. (1991, Nihon seimei).

Formerly, *otoshidama* was a custom of exchanging gifts for the New Year among nobles and warriors in the late Muromachi Era (1336−1573).

Monetary gifts to children became more prevalent in the Meiji Era over a century ago.

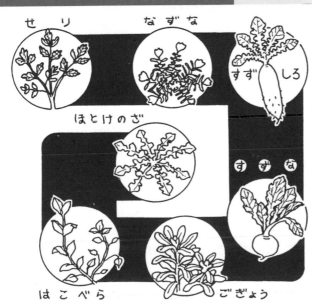

Hatsumōde 初詣

Many people make their first visit to a shrine or a temple soon after the temple bells have pealed out the old year, or during the first week of the New Year. They throw money into an offertory box and pray for good fortune. After worshipping, they buy a good luck talisman or a sacred arrow with white feathers. It is fun to draw lots for a written fortune bearing a Chinese character meaning either good or bad luck. After reading the fortune, people tie the slip of paper to a branch of a tree in the shrine precincts for better luck.

The seven spring herbs are Japanese parsley, shepherd's purse, cutweed, chickweed, turnip, henbit, and garden radish. It is customary to eat rice gruel made with these seven herbs of spring on the seventh day of the New Year's holiday.

It is believed to prevent colds and other diseases.

This custom dates back to the Heian Period. Today a package containing all seven herbs is readily available in supermarkets.

Haru no Nanakusa 春の七草

せ　り　　　な　ず　な　　　すず　しろ
ほとけのざ　　　すずな
はこべら　　　ごぎょう

11

Seijinshiki 成人式

Coming-of-Age Day was established after World War II to honor young people who have reached the age of 20 during the past year as new members of society. They get all the rights of citizenship, including the right to vote, and should be ready to make their own way with responsibility in society.

Congratulatory ceremonies are held throughout the country. Many young women attend in *kimono* and photographs are taken to remember this special day.

はっけよい！

十一月場所（じゅういちがつばしょ）
福岡（ふくおか）
三月場所（さんがつばしょ）
大阪（おおさか）
七月場所（しちがつばしょ）
名古屋（なごや）
一月場所（いちがつばしょ）
五月場所（ごがつばしょ）
九月場所（くがつばしょ）
東京（とうきょう）

Sumō 相撲

Sumō is Japan's national sport and has existed since ancient times. Professional *sumō* appeared in the Edo Period.

In *sumō*, two wrestlers face off in the middle of a *dohyō* ring measuring 4.55 meters in diameter. Every action, such as scattering purifying salt on the ring, is part of *sumō's* ancient tradition.

There are 70 different ways to win, such as *oshidashi* (push out), *uwatenage* (over-arm throw), *yoritaoshi* (frontal crush-out) or *yorikiri* (frontal force-out). *Sumō* wrestlers are ranked according to their results. *Yokozuna* (grand champion), *Ōzeki* (champion), and *Sekiwake* (junior champion) are the top three ranks. They wrestle with several ranked competitors during the 15 day-tournament, and a winner is decided.

Sumō wrestling tournaments have been held six times a year since 1958.

The achievements of a few foreign wrestlers have gradually internationalized the appeal of *sumō*. The number of *sumō* fans is increasing, not only among Japanese, but also non-Japanese.

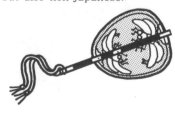

JANUARY 1 月

睦_む月_つ_き

Mutsuki means "Family Gathering Month."
This is month for families and kinfolk to get together
and enjoy each other's company.

We call the 1st of January *Ganjitsu*; to the Japanese people, this is the most important day of the year's beginning.

People decorate their entranceways and gates for the New Year. In the past, the decorations were *kadomatsu* or *shimekazari*, but today's decorations are simpler, like a wreath on the door.

The morning of *Ganjitsu* is called *Gantan*. At *Gantan* families drink *o-toso* together and eat *o-zoni* and *osechi* in celebration of the New Year. Children receive *otoshidama* from their parents. It is customary to make the year's first visit to a temple or a shrine to pray for happiness in the New Year. Although these are the main customs of the New Year, nowadays increasing numbers of people spend the New Year at hotels, in spas, at ski resorts or in foreign countries.

On New Year's Day, New Year's greeting cards are delivered all at once. Many of them have a picture of the *eto* of the year or a family photograph printed along with New Year's greetings. Looking at these cards is one of the pleasures of the New Year.

During *Shōgatsu sanganichi*, which is January 1st, 2nd and 3d, banks, government offices, and nearly all companies and stores are closed. On these days, we go around on New Year's visits to the homes of our friends, relatives and our superiors at the office or company.

The 4th of January is the first day of work for government and municipal offices. Companies also reopen for business on this day after New Year's vacation.

On the 7th, it is traditional to eat *nanakusagayu*. *Nanakusagayu* is rice porridge with seven spring herbs in it. It is said that by eating *nanakusagayu*, one can stay healthy for the whole year.

The 15th of January is "Coming-of-Age Day." This is a day to congratulate people who have turned 20 years old, and to hold special Coming-of-Age ceremonies.

In the middle of the month, the year's first *sumō* wrestling tournament is held at Ryogoku National Sport Indoor Arena in Tokyo, and a winner is decided after 15 days of tough competition.

Around the 21st is *Daikan*, the coldest day of the year according to the lunar calendar. The merry mood of *Matsu no uchi* is over, and the weather turns bitter cold.

2月
FEBRUARY

如月（きさらぎ）

3日 節分（せつぶん）
4日 立春（りっしゅん）
11日 建国記念日（けんこくきねんび）

　2月は1年で一番寒い月です。

　北海道や日本海側は雪が多いので、各地で「雪まつり」が行われます。札幌の雪まつりは特に有名で、数メートルもある像や建物のもけいを雪で作ります。このまつりには観光客が日本各地からだけでなく、外国からもおとずれます。

5　西高東低の気圧配置がゆるむ中旬からは、東京でも雪がふることがあります。雪になれない東京では、つもると交通が混乱したり、こおった雪ですべってけが人が出たりします。

　スキーは今の若者に人気がある冬のスポーツの一つです。休日になると各地のスキー場がにぎわい、リフトには長い行列ができます。

10　2月は受験シーズンです。日本では大学や高校と、私立や国立の中学には入学試験があります。これらの試験はどれも競争がきびしいので、「受験地獄」といわれています。

　3日は「節分（せつぶん）」です。こよみの上で季節が冬と春とにわかれる日です。鬼を追い払って新しい春を迎えるために、節分には「豆まき」をします。神社やお寺では「年男（としおとこ）」「年女（としおんな）」が豆まきを行い、夜になると各家庭で「鬼は外、福は
15　内」といって豆をまきます。年令と同じ数だけ豆を食べると、1年間健康であると信じられています。

　4日は「立春（りっしゅん）」で、春の始まりを意味します。気温は低くても梅や水仙の花が咲き始め、冷たい空気の中を花の香りがただよいます。

20　中旬以後には「春一番」がふきあれます。これは春をつげる強い南風です。こうして一歩一歩やって来る春を人々は心待ちにします。

梅一輪（うめいちりん）　一輪（いちりん）ほどの　あたたかさ　　　　　嵐雪

漢字のよみかた

一番 いちばん	寒い さむ	北海道 ほっかいどう	日本海側 にほんかいがわ	雪 ゆき	各地 かくち
行われます おこな	札幌 さっぽろ	特に とく	有名で ゆうめい	数メートル すう	像 ぞう
建物 たてもの	作ります つく	観光客 かんこうきゃく	5 西高東低 せいこうとうてい	気圧配置 きあつはいち	中旬 ちゅうじゅん
交通 こうつう	混乱したり こんらん	出たり で	若者 わかもの	人気 にんき	一つ ひと
休日 きゅうじつ	スキー場 じょう	行列 ぎょうれつ	10 受験シーズン じゅけん	私立 しりつ	国立 こくりつ
入学試験 にゅうがくしけん	競争 きょうそう	受験地獄 じゅけんじごく	3日 みっか	節分 せつぶん	季節 きせつ
鬼 おに	追い払って お はら	迎える むか	豆まき まめ	神社 じんじゃ	15 お寺 てら
年男 としおとこ	年女 としおんな	行い おこな	夜 よる	各家庭 かくかてい	鬼は外 おに そと
福は内 ふく うち	年令 ねんれい	同じ数 おな かず	健康 けんこう	信じられて しん	4日 よっか
立春 りっしゅん	始まり はじ	意味します いみ	気温 きおん	低くても ひく	梅 うめ
水仙 すいせん	咲き始め さ はじ	冷たい つめ	空気 くうき	香り かお	20 以後 いご
春一番 はるいちばん	強い つよ	南風 みなみかぜ	一歩一歩 いっぽ いっぽ	来る く	心待ち こころま
一輪 いちりん	嵐雪 らんせつ				

Winter Weather Chart
冬の気圧配置図

Typical winter weather chart shows high pressure over the Asian continent to the west, and low pressure east of Japan at sea. This pressure pattern causes heavy snow on the Japan Sea coastal areas and sunny dry weather on the Pacific coastal areas.

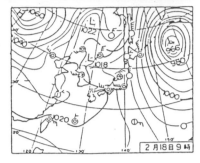

Snow Shoveling off Roof
雪おろし

It snows heavily on the Japan Sea coastal areas and Hokkaido, where snow stays for months. Roofs are pitched to get rid of piled-up snow, but still it is necessary to shovel the snow off the roof so its weight will not crush the house.

Snowfall in Tokyo
東京の雪

Tokyo people are not prepared for snow. Children and adults have difficulty commuting on snowy mornings. Because of the snow on the ground, people slip and get hurt, and ambulances are busy all day.

Kamakura
かまくら

Kamakura is one of children's winter pleasures, in snow country. The most famous *kamakura* festival is held in Yokote, Akita Prefecture, on February 15th and 16th. *Kamakura*, igloo-like snow houses, are built on roadsides, with an altar for the water god inside. On the evening of the 15th, children gather inside, light candles and have rice cakes and *amazake*.

Snow Festival　　　雪まつり

The Sapporo Snow Festival is held for one week in early February. In the center of the city over 200 big snow statues are lined up, some of them as tall as 15 meters.

There are two other sites, one at Susukino for ice statues and the other at Makomanai for bigger statues. Snow statues and replicas at Odori Park in Sapporo are lit up at night.

Mamemaki

豆まき

On February 3rd huge crowds are attracted to watch celebrities who happen to be *toshiotoko* or *toshion'na* — born under the same zodiac animal as the current year — throw beans at big temples and shrines. At home parents and children throw beans in the living room, out from entranceway, etc., saying "*Oni wa soto, fuku wa uchi.*"

えと
The 60-Year Cycle

The concept of *jikkan* and *jūnishi* (also called *kan shi*) was derived from China in the 6th Century, and has been used to denote the year of the Japanese calendar. For example, 1992 is the Year of the Monkey.

Jikkan (pairs of 5 elements) and *jūnishi* (the 12 animal zodiac signs) are combined to make the 60-year cycle. People often say, "I was born in the year of *saru* (monkey), or *i* (boar)," or one of the other zodiac animals. Every 12 years your *eto* year turns around, and you will be *toshi--otoko* or *toshion'na*. After you go through the 60-year cycle, you will have a big celebration on your 60th birthday. This is called *kanreki*. (See "Celebration of Longevity" on p.61)

College Entrance Examinations　　大学入試

Why are entrance exams so competitive? Because people think a diploma from a top university means a passport to good lifetime employment. So young children start studying at *juku* after regular school hours, with their ultimate goal to go to a good university.

Usually examinees for high schools apply to a few schools but ones for college apply to ten on average.

Every year over one million high school graduates take entrance examinations to 4-year colleges or 2-year junior colleges. In 1991, 64% passed; those who fail study at "*yobikō*" or "*juku*" schools one more year and try again the next year. They are called "*rōnin*," and in recent years there are around 300,000 of them annually.

Eventually 37.7% of high school graduates go on to colleges. (Source : *The Asahi*, 1991)

俳句
Haiku

Haiku is perhaps the shortest poetic form in the world, consisting of three lines of 5, 7 and 5 syllables. The rhythm of 5, 7 and 5 syllables has a pleasant sound in the Japanese language.

Haiku originated from the literary form called *haikai-renga* of the 14th to 16th Centuries. *Haikai-renga* consists of 5, 7, 5, 7 and 7 syllables. The first three lines developed as *haikai*, later becoming *haiku*.

Ume ichi-rin*	(6 syllables)	One twig of plum blossoms,
Ichirin hodo no	(7 syllables)	One twigful of
Atatakasa	(5 syllables)	Warmth.

This *haiku* by Hattori Ransetsu has been loved by the Japanese since the Edo Era. When the first sign of spring is noticed, people often quote it. *Haiku* like this one convey rich imagery in very few words. The secret is the use of *kigo*, words typical of the season. Each *haiku* has to have one and one only *kigo*. These seasonal words are collected in a book called *Saijiki*, and poets refer to this book to use *kigo* appropriately.

Haiku is still popular, and 10 million people write them in Japan. Newspapers have *haiku* columns, and poets form groups, each publishing their own periodicals. People in other countries write *haiku* in their own language.

* Here it should be 5 syllables, but 6 is allowed as exception.

("N" forms 1 syllable in Japanese language.)

FEBRUARY 　2 月

如 き
月 さ
　 ら
　 ぎ

Kisaragi means to wear layers of clothing, one over another. The name of the month is homonymous to "着 －更－着 [ki-sara-ki]" meaning "wear-over-wear."

February is the coldest month of the year.

Snowfall is heavy in Hokkaido and the Japan Sea coastal areas, and snow festivals are held there during this month. The Sapporo Snow Festival in Hokkaido is especially famous for its snow statues many meters high, and its huge ice and snow replicas of famous buildings. People come to see them not only from Japan's mainland, but from all over the world.

The atmospheric pressure pattern of "high in the west, low in the east" prevails through most of the winter, but this changes after the middle of the month when it may snow even in Tokyo. Tokyo people are not accustomed to snow, and sometimes traffic is paralyzed or people slip on the ice and get hurt.

Skiing is a popular winter sport among young people. Ski areas are crowded on weekends and holidays, and lines are long at the chairlifts.

February is also the time for tests. In Japan there are entrance examinations for high schools, universities and colleges, and also for some private and national junior high schools. These tests are so difficult to pass that the experience is called "examination hell."

February the 3rd is *Setsubun*. On the lunar calendar, this is the turning point from winter to spring. To celebrate the coming of spring and drive away evil spirits, a bean-throwing is held. At Shinto shrines and Buddhist temples, *toshiotoko* and *toshion'na** throw beans; at home in the evening, families throw beans and shout, "Evil spirits outside, good luck within!" If you eat the same number of beans as your age, it is believed, you will stay healthy throughout the year.

The next day, February the 4th, is *Risshun*, which means the first day of spring. Although the mercury stays low, plum blossoms and daffodils begin to bud and their fragrance floats in the chilly air.

After midmonth, *haruichiban* rages through the country. This is the first southern storm of the year.

People long for the coming of spring.

> One twig of plum blossoms,
> One twigful of
> Warmth. 　　　—Ransetsu

* Men and women born under the same zodiac sign as the current year

３月
MARCH

弥生（やよい）

3日　ひなまつり
12日　お水取り（みずと）
21日ころ　春分の日（しゅんぶん ひ）

　　3月は「弥生（やよい）」ともよばれます。「やよい」とはますます成長するという意味です。

　　3月3日は「ひなまつり」です。女の子のいる家ではひな人形をかざり、ももの花やなの花を生けます。ちらし寿司、はまぐりの吸い物、ひなあられや白
5 酒などを用意して、友だちや親戚の人をまねいて、ひなまつりをします。

　　また、3日は「耳の日」です。アラビア数字の3が耳の形に似ていることと、3がミと読めることから、ミミの日になりました。耳の健康を考える日です。

　　日本の学校は4月に始まって3月に終わるので、この月には卒業式、終業式が行われます。卒業式では幼稚園から大学までの、最終学年の生徒たちは卒業
10 証書をもらいます。式の後、長い間お世話になった先生に感謝の気持ちを表して、謝恩会が開かれます。父母が参加することもあります。卒業式や終業式が終わると、学校は春休みになります。

　　会社や銀行も3月が決算期にあたるところが多くあり、「所得税確定申告」の月でもあります。このように3月は1年の区切りの月なので、転勤、転校、
15 引越が多い季節です。

　　12日の真夜中には奈良の東大寺二月堂で「お水取り」が行われます。これは関西地方では春をつげる大切な行事の一つです。

　　21日ごろは「春分の日」です。昼と夜の長さが同じになる日です。この前後1週間を「お彼岸（ひがん）」といって、家族そろってお墓参りをします。
20 　「暑さ寒さも彼岸まで」と昔からいうように、春のお彼岸が来ると寒さが終わって春になり、秋のお彼岸が来ると、暑さが終わって秋になります。

漢字のよみかた

弥生 やよい	成長する せいちょう	意味 いみ	3日 みっか	人形 にんぎょう	生けます い
ちらし寿司 ずし	吸い物 す もの	白酒 しろざけ	5 用意して ようい	友だち とも	親戚 しんせき
数字 すうじ	形 かたち	似ている に	健康 けんこう	考える かんが	始って はじま
終わる お	卒業式 そつぎょうしき	終業式 しゅうぎょうしき	行われます おこな	幼稚園 ようちえん	最終学年 さいしゅうがくねん
生徒 せいと	卒業証書 そつぎょうしょうしょ	10 式 しき	後 あと	お世話 せわ	感謝 かんしゃ
気持ち きも	表して あらわ	謝恩会 しゃおんかい	開かれます ひら	父母 ふぼ	参加する さんか
決算期 けっさんき	所得税確定申告 しょとくぜいかくていしんこく	区切り く ぎ	転勤 てんきん	転校 てんこう
15 引越 ひっこし	季節 きせつ	真夜中 まよなか	奈良 なら	東大寺 とうだいじ	二月堂 にがつどう
お水取り みずと	関西地方 かんさいちほう	大切な たいせつ	行事 ぎょうじ	一つ ひと	春分の日 しゅんぶん ひ
昼 ひる	夜 よる	同じ おな	前後 ぜんご	お彼岸 ひがん	家族 かぞく
お墓参り はかまい	20 暑さ あつ	寒さ さむ	昔 むかし	来る く

21

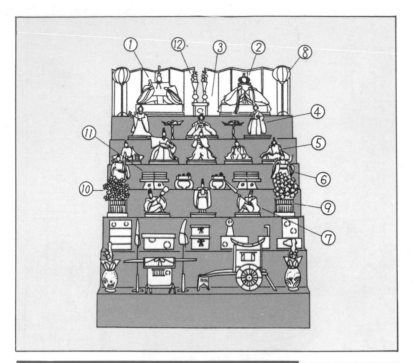

Hinamatsuri
ひなまつり

The original festival, mentioned in *The Tale of Genji*, written in the beginning of the 11th Century, was to protect people from evil. Everyone made his own statue or doll, wrote his name on it, and floated it down a stream hoping evil fortune would float away with the statue.

Hinaningyō   ひな人形

Traditional display for *hinamatsuri*. (Above)

In the middle of the Edo Period (1603-1867), people made elaborate dolls that they displayed only on red-felt-carpeted special steps inside the house, as you see today.

The set is made up of fifteen dolls in formal classical court costumes — Emperor ① and Empress ② on the top shelf in front of a golden folding screen ③, three ladies-in-waiting ④, five musicians ⑤, two retainers ⑥ and three guards ⑦. Two *bonbori* lanterns ⑧, a miniature cherry blossom tree ⑨, and an orange tree ⑩ lend a festive air on the steps. Special *hinamatsuri* goodies such as colorful *hishimochi* (diamondshaped rice cakes) ⑪, *shirozake* ⑫ and *hina arare* are offered. Miniature furniture, lacquered tableware and vehicles on the lower shelves symbolize a bridal dowry.

Nagashibina
流しびな

Now the original custom of a thousand years ago remains only in limited parts of Japan as *nagashibina*. A pair of paper dolls are laid in a small straw boat with peach blossoms and rice cakes and set afloat on the river, to carry away evil with them.

Tachibina
立ちびな

The original form of the handmade paper figures in standing position remains today. The *hina* couple is called *"tachi bina."* Because of limited space in many houses today, some families display just *tachibina* dolls in a glass case, or simply a scroll with a *tachibina* pattern.

Omizutori
お水取り

Omizutori, the spectacular feast of water and fire, takes place on March the 12th. It has been celebrated since the middle of the 8th Century. At midnight the festival reaches its climax. On the veranda of the temple,

young monks wave huge torches, showering sparks down onto the worshipers below. At two o'clock in the morning, one of the torch bearers proceeds to the holy well, Wakasai Well*, inside Nigatsudo Hall. There the secret water-drawing ceremony is performed by chosen priests. A bucket of holy water is carried back to the main hall to be of-fered to the Great Buddha. It is believed that those worshipers who catch a "flake" of fire from the torches are free from evil spirits and disease for a whole year.

* This water comes underground direct from Wakasa Province, Fukui Prefecture, so they say, and the well was named "Wa-kasai."

ごろ合わせ
Puns with Numerals

Since we can read each numeral in several ways in Japanese, we enjoy puns with numerals.

Multiple ways of reading numerals help us to remember big figures such as telephone numbers or historic years. They also give meanings to dates such as:

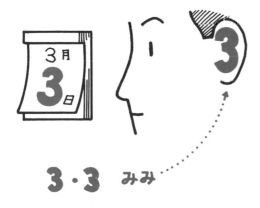

3月3日	3・3	み・み	耳の日 Ears Day
6月4日	6・4	む・し	虫歯予防デー Prevent Tooth Decay Day
8月7日	8・7	は・な	鼻の日 Nose Day
23日	2・3	ふ・み	ふみ(手紙)の日 Letter-Writing Day

Some hospitals and hotels avoid numbering rooms with "4" or "42," which can be read "shi" and "shi-ni," meaning "death."

Visiting the Family Graves お墓まいり

The old Japanese folklore belief of worshiping the souls of ancestors was combined with the Buddhist belief that Heaven lies due west. People started to visit their family graves, so they say, on the Equinox, when the sun sets due west. This custom exists neither in China nor India.

At the graveyard, people sweep around the gravestones and wash them. After the cleaning, they offer flowers, incense sticks and food and drinks which their ancestors loved. Each person pours water over the stone, and prays. They say the dead are always feeling thirsty, so the water soothes them.

Sotsugyōshiki
卒業式

The highlight of a graduation ceremony held at a *kōdō*, an auditorium, is "the presentation of certificates." At elementary schools and middle schools, the class teacher calls the names of the graduating students one by one, and each student is handed a diploma on the platform by a headmaster with a brief personal comment. Some big schools and universities rent a public hall. In such a huge ceremony a representative receives all the certificates on behalf of his or her classmates. Caps and gowns like those seen in the West are rare in Japan. College graduates wear suits, though many girls still wear *kimono* and solid colored *hakama*, which makes the outfit formal.

Tenkin
転 勤

Transfer season causes a fuss among some families. Because of several reasons such as their children's educational situation or care of elderly parents, some fathers today are forced to do "*tanshinfunin*" — to go to a new post alone apart from the family.

House-moving is a big business in Japan today, and companies offer a variety of services to answer many different needs of such customers. The "rent-all system" — renting furniture, electrical goods and daily essentials in a package deal is one service offered for these "bachelor fathers."

MARCH 3 月

弥や
よ
生い | *Yayoi* means "to grow more and more." Japanese "Groundhog Day," *Keichitsu*, is around March the 6th. On this day, the creatures come out of the ground, birds begin to sing, and flowers and trees start to bloom.

The month of March is also called *Yayoi*. *Yayoi* means to grow more and more.

March 3rd is the *Hina* Doll Festival. Families who have daughters display a set of *hina* dolls and arrangements of peach-blossoms and rape-blossoms. Special foods such as *chirashizushi*, clear soup with clams, *hina arare* and white, sweet *sake* are prepared, and friends and relatives are invited to celebrate the *Hina* Doll Festival.

The 3rd is also "Ears Day." The shape of the Arabic numeral 3 resembles that of an ear, and the numeral 3 can be read in Japanese as *mi*, so March 3rd [3/3] sounds like *mi-mi** and the day is called *Mimi no Hi* — "Ears Day." This is the day to think about the care of the ears.

The school year in Japan begins in April and ends in March, so this is the month that commencement and school closing ceremonies are held. At commencement ceremonies, graduating students from kindergarten through university receive certificates. After the ceremony, the students give a *shaonkai* party in honor of their teachers, to show appreciation for their guidance. Parents sometimes participate as well. When the graduation and school closing ceremonies are over, spring holidays begin.

Many companies and banks have designated March as the month for settling the year's accounts, and it is also the month for filing income tax returns. As March is the end of the fiscal year, it is the busy season for transfers — jobs, schools, and moving to new houses.

Late in the night of March the 12th, *Omizutori*, the Water-Drawing Ceremony, is held at Nigatsudo Hall of Todaiji Temple in Nara. In the Kansai area of Japan, this is an important event to herald the coming of spring.

The Spring Equinox comes around the 21st. This is the day when daylight and nighttime become exactly equal. The week around this day is called *O-higan*, and families go together to visit the graves of their ancestors.

An old proverb says, "Neither heat nor cold lasts over the Equinox." By the time of the Spring Equinox, the winter cold is over and spring is here; by the time of the Autumn Equinox, the summer heat is over and autumn has arrived.

* The Japanese word for "ear"

25

4月
APRIL

卯月
（うづき）

29日　みどりの日

　4月になると気温が上がってあたたかな日がふえます。北海道や東北地方はまだ雪が残っているところもありますが、関東地方以南では桜ややまぶきなどの春の花が咲き始めます。

　日本では学校や会社の1年は4月に始まります。学校では始業式をして新学期を迎えます。新入生のためには入学式を行い、校長先生の話やそれぞれの先生の紹介があります。小学1年生は両親や祖父母から新しいランドセルやつくえを買ってもらいます。

　会社では入社式をします。新しいスーツを着た新入社員に社長が激励のことばをおくります。入社式の前後に、新入社員は2、3日から3か月間くらいの研修を受けます。

　プロ野球の開幕も4月です。日本では大人も子供も野球が大好きで、4月のプロ野球開幕戦にはファンがたくさん集まります。

　また、4月は「お花見」の季節です。お花見は桜を楽しむ伝統的な春の行事です。桜は南の暖かい沖縄から咲き始め、九州、四国、本州と咲き出し、北海道では5月初めごろ咲きます。このころになると桜の開花時期を示す「桜前線」の動きのようすを毎日、テレビの天気予報で知ることができます。桜が咲くと、人々はお弁当やお酒を持って桜の名所をおとずれ、花の下を歩いたり、食べたり、飲んだりします。夜空に桜の花が浮かび上がる「夜桜」も風情があります。その下で歌ったり、おどったりして、夜遅くまでにぎやかにすごす人もいます。1週間ぐらいで桜の花は終わり、若葉の季節が始まります。

　29日は「みどりの日」で、祝日です。4月の末から5月の初めのこの週には、4日間の祝日のほかに、振替休日が加わることがあり、大型連休となります。

漢字のよみかた

気温（きおん）	上（あ）がって	北海道（ほっかいどう）	東北地方（とうほくちほう）	雪（ゆき）	残（のこ）っている
関東地方（かんとうちほう）	以南（いなん）	桜（さくら）	咲（さ）き始（はじ）め	始（はじ）まります	始業式（しぎょうしき）
新学期（しんがっき）	迎（むか）えます	新入生（しんにゅうせい）	入学式（にゅうがくしき）	行（おこな）い	校長先生（こうちょうせんせい）
紹介（しょうかい）	両親（りょうしん）	祖父母（そふぼ）	入社式（にゅうしゃしき）	新入社員（しんにゅうしゃいん）	激励（げきれい）
前後（ぜんご）	2、3日（に さんにち）	3か月間（さんげつかん）	研修（けんしゅう）	受（う）けます	プロ野球（やきゅう）
開幕（かいまく）	大人（おとな）	子供（こども）	大好（だいす）き	開幕戦（かいまくせん）	集（あつ）まり
お花見（はなみ）	季節（きせつ）	楽（たの）しむ	伝統的（でんとうてき）な	行事（ぎょうじ）	暖（あたた）かい
沖縄（おきなわ）	九州（きゅうしゅう）	四国（しこく）	本州（ほんしゅう）	咲（さ）き出（だ）し	初（はじ）め
開花時期（かいかじき）	桜前線（さくらぜんせん）	動（うご）き	天気予報（てんきよほう）	お弁当（べんとう）	お酒（さけ）
名所（めいしょ）	夜空（よぞら）	浮（う）かび上（あ）がる	夜桜（よざくら）	風情（ふぜい）	歌（うた）ったり
夜遅（よるおそ）く	終（お）わり	若葉（わかば）	祝日（しゅくじつ）	末（すえ）	4日間（よっかかん）
振替休日（ふりかえきゅうじつ）	加（くわ）わる	大型連休（おおがたれんきゅう）			

27

Nyūshashiki 入社式

Most companies hold an entrance ceremony for their freshman employees. After, or sometimes before the entrance ceremony, these new employees are required to go through a series of training sessions that often run for more than a month. During the training sessions, such information as general operations of the company, personal health management, and etiquette in the business world is given to the young men and women, who have just graduated from school.

日本の学校制度
School System in Japan

In Japan, education is highly valued. Although nine years' school education is required for all Japanese children, more than 95 of 100 students go on to the high school level. Many parents want their children to get a university or college diploma, so university entrance examinations are very competitive. There are 507 four-year universities and colleges and 593 two-year junior colleges; about 230 of those are public schools. Colleges and universities are concentrated in the Tokyo area, 161 of 507 four-year colleges and universities and 143 of 593 two-year junior colleges were in the Tokyo area in 1990.

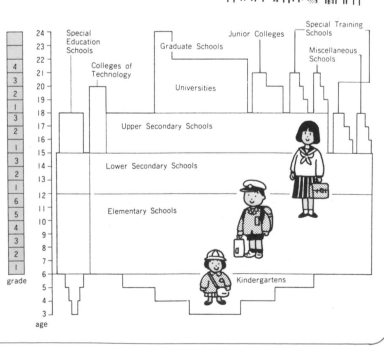

Source : Ministry of Education, Science and Culture

O-hanami　　　お花見

The cherry blossom is designated the "national flower" of Japan. Since ancient times, the most loved flower in Japan has been the cherry blossom. It has appeared in many literary works, and the cherry blossom design has been extremely popular for almost anything in Japanese life.

As the proverb says, "*Hana yori dango*" (Better to eat sweet dumplings than to view the flowers), people enjoy eating and drinking under cherry trees and have fun at *o-hanami*.

Sakura Zensen

桜前線

After close observation of the trees at 120 designated locations all over Japan, the Meteorological Agency releases a forecast and makes an official announcement when the cherry trees bloom. The line connecting points where cherry trees are forecast to bloom on the same day is called "*Sakura zensen*," the cherry blossom front. Even in today's busy life, the Japanese talk about cherry blossoms in their daily conversation at this time of year, and they go out to view and enjoy the cherry flowers.

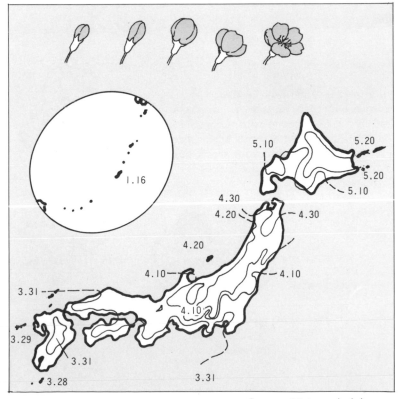

Source : Meteorogical Agency

Professional Baseball Games
日本のプロ野球

Baseball is widely played and very popular in Japan. The game was first introduced to the Japanese in 1873; it was enjoyed as a students' sport until 1937, when the first professional baseball teams were formed. The professional baseball games became especially popular after World War Ⅱ, the period when the influence of American culture has been strong in many phases of Japanese life. Today, there are two leagues in professional baseball, the Central League and the Pacific League, each having six teams. The Japan Series is held at the end of each year's baseball season with the winners of each league competing. Each year, more than 20,000,000 go to baseball stadiums to watch pro games.

春の味、春の野山
Spring Food, Flora and Fauna

さんさい	Edible wild plants, especially young shoots that come out in spring
たけのこ	Bamboo shoots
ひなあられ	Sugar coated rice crispies for Hina Doll Festival
白酒	Sweet, white rice wine brewed from *sake* and rice malt
桜もち	Sweet, pink-colored rice cake wrapped with a cherry leaf
ぼたもち	Sweetened rice dumpling coated with sweet bean paste
花見だんご	Small sweet rice-flour dumplings mixed with sweet bean paste
ちまき	Dumpling of sweet rice wrapped in bamboo leaves
かしわもち	Sweet rice cake wrapped in an oak leaf
はまぐり	Clams
さより	Halfbeak, a spring fish
つばき	Camellia
じんちょうげ	Daphne
なの花	Rape blossoms
たんぽぽ	Dandelion
れんげ	Clover-like grass with pink flowers
すみれ	Violet
つつじ	Azalea
ぼたん	Peony
ふじ	Wisteria
もんしろちょう	Cabbage white, a kind of butterfly
おたまじゃくし	Tadpole
ひばり	Skylark

APRIL 4 月

卯 う
づ
月 き

Uzuki is month in which *unohana*, small white flowers, are in full bloom on the hedges.

As April comes, the mercury rises and there are more and more warm days. Although snow may still be found in Hokkaido and Tohoku, in places south of the Kanto area cherry trees, *yamabuki*, and other spring flowers are blossoming.

In Japan schools and corporations begin their year in April. Each school greets the new term with an opening ceremony. For students beginning their first year at a new school, there is an entrance ceremony, in which the school principal gives a speech and teachers are introduced. First graders in elementary school, starting school for the first time in their lives, get a new *randoseru** and a new desk from their parents or grandparents.

Businesses hold entrance ceremonies as well. The company president makes a speech offering words of encouragement to the entering employees, all dressed in their new business suits. Around the time of the entrance ceremony, the new employees begin a period of training that lasts from two or three days to three months.

The opening of the professional baseball season is also in April. In Japan, both adults and children love baseball, and fans throng to the season opener in April.

And April is the season for flower viewing. *O-hanami* is a traditional spring event of enjoying cherry blossoms. Cherry trees begin blooming first in warm Okinawa, then the blooms come out in Kyushu, Shikoku and Honshu. In Hokkaido, *sakura* season is early May. Around this time on the television weather reports, you can watch the progress of the "cherry blossom front," which tells the time the cherry trees will bloom. When the *sakura* are in bloom, people take *o-bentō* lunches and *sake* to some spot famous for the beauty of its cherry blossoms, and they walk and have a picnic or a drinking party under the cherry trees. *Yozakura*, white cherry blossoms outlined against the night sky, have a special beauty. People stay out until late evening singing and dancing gaily. The cherry blossoms last about a week, and then young leaves grow quickly to cover the tree with green.

The 29th of April is Greenery Day, a national holiday. In the week from the end of April to the beginning of May, there are four national holidays; sometimes a designated holiday is added, so it becomes a "big scale holiday week."

* A backpack-type book bag

5月
MAY

皐月（さつき）

3日　憲法記念日（けんぽうきねんび）
4日　国民の休日（こくみんきゅうじつ）
5日　子供の日（こどものひ）
第2日曜日　母の日（ははのひ）

　　日本の5月はさわやかで、新緑の美しい季節です。このころの晴天を五月晴（さつきば）れとよびます。多くの学校で遠足や運動会が行われます。

　　5月1日はメーデーです。日本ではこの日は働く者の祭典として各地で催し物が行われます。

5　　3日は「憲法記念日」、4日は「国民の休日」、5日は「子供の日」で、三連休となります。

　　「みどりの日」から「子供の日」までのこの週を「ゴールデンウィーク」といい、友だちや家族で旅行したり、潮干狩りやスポーツを楽しみます。おおぜいの人が戸外に出かけるので、行楽地や道路はどこでも大混雑です。

10　　正月、夏休みとともにゴールデンウィークにも、たくさんの人たちが海外旅行をします。今では日本の海外旅行者は年間1000万人（1990年現在）をこえています。

　　子供の日は昔、「端午の節句（たんごのせっく）」といわれ、男の子の成長を祝う日でした。現在は、男の子と女の子の成長を祝う日になっています。今でも男の子のいる家

15　ではこいのぼりを立てたり、五月人形やかぶとをかざります。また、しょうぶ湯に入ったり、ちまきやかしわもちを食べる風習があります。

　　第2日曜日は「母の日」です。この日にはお母さんに赤いカーネーションやプレゼントをおくり、感謝の気持ちを表します。

　　5月は新茶の季節です。「八十八夜」のころの新芽で作ったお茶は香りがよく、

20　うまみがあるので、特に喜ばれます。

漢字のよみかた

新緑（しんりょく）	美しい（うつくしい）	季節（きせつ）	晴天（せいてん）	五月晴れ（さつきばれ）	遠足（えんそく）
運動会（うんどうかい）	行われます（おこなわれます）	1日（ついたち）	働く者（はたらくもの）	祭典（さいてん）	各地（かくち）
催し物（もよおしもの）	5 3日（みっか）	憲法記念日（けんぽうきねんび）	4日（よっか）	国民の休日（こくみんのきゅうじつ）	5日（いつか）
子供の日（こどものひ）	三連休（さんれんきゅう）	友だち（とも）	家族（かぞく）	旅行したり（りょこう）	潮干狩り（しおひがり）
楽しみます（たのしみます）	戸外（こがい）	出かける（でかける）	行楽地（こうらくち）	道路（どうろ）	大混雑（だいこんざつ）
10 海外旅行（かいがいりょこう）	旅行者（りょこうしゃ）	年間（ねんかん）	現在（げんざい）	昔（むかし）	端午の節句（たんごのせっく）
成長（せいちょう）	祝う（いわう）	15 五月人形（ごがつにんぎょう）	しょうぶ湯（ゆ）	風習（ふうしゅう）	第2日曜日（だいにちようび）
赤い（あかい）	感謝（かんしゃ）	気持ち（きもち）	表します（あらわします）	新茶（しんちゃ）	八十八夜（はちじゅうはちや）
新芽（しんめ）	作った（つくった）	香り（かおり）	20 特に（とくに）	喜ばれます（よころばれます）	

Gogatsuningyō

五月人形

Toward Boy's Day *gogatsuningyō*, warrior dolls, and *kabuto*, warriors' helmets, are displayed at home, in the hope that the boys will grow as strong and healthy as warriors. But recently only *kabuto* are displayed because city houses and apartments have limited space.

kashiwamochi

Koinobori

こいのぼり

Even now families with boys hoist *koinobori*, carp streamers. This originated from the Chinese legend of strong carp that could fight their way up the Yellow River to become dragons.

The largest *koinobori* measure 5 to 6 meters, but 1-to 2-meter *koinobori* sell best because many people put them up on the balconies of their apartment houses.

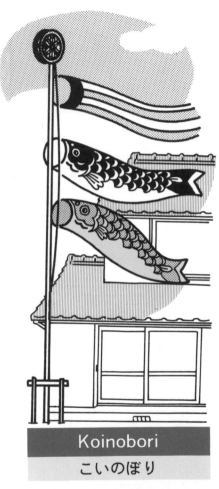

Shōbuyu   しょうぶ湯

On *Tango no Sekku* (Boy's Day) iris and *yomogi* leaves decorate the eaves of houses, and an iris leaf bath is prepared because it is believed to drive away evil spirits. On this day *sentō*, public bath houses, prepare iris baths, and children are admitted free.

Warrior's Helmet　かぶと　　おり紙

1 2 3 4

5 6 7 8

9

1. Make a triangle.
2. Fold again to make another triangle, and open.
3. With folded edge, fold again to make two triangles along center line.
4. Take top layer and make a triangle, one on each side.
5. Take inner edge and fold down equally on both sides away from you.
6. Take top layer. Fold upward so point is halfway from top (not all the way to top).
7. With the same piece, fold lower layer up again.
8. To finish, tuck bottom flap inside.

Clam Gathering at Low Tide　潮干狩り

The spring tide occurs around Golden Week, and the water temperature has risen by this time. So people like to be on the beach, and clam gathering at low tide is one of the typical diversions of this season.

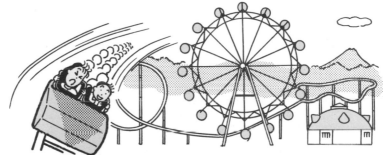

Amusement Parks　　遊園地

Amusement parks are the most popular destinations for both young and old. People rush to Tokyo Disneyland especially. In 1991 more than half a million people had fun there during Golden Week. 100,000 came each day on peak days.

Chatsumi
茶つみ

Young tea leaves are picked around the 88th day after *Risshun*. These are called *ichiban-cha*, first tea leaves, and they have a wonderful flavor and fragrance. Tea leaves traditionally were picked by hand, but because of the labor shortage, the work is now done by machine.

Narita Airport is crowded during Golden Week with Japanese tourists who travel to various parts of the world. Hawaii, Guam and Southeast Asia are their favorite destinations, but some also visit faraway places like South America, Africa or even the Antarctic.

Overseas Travel　海外旅行

In 1964 when restrictions on overseas travel were lifted, the number of travellers was 130,000. Now about 10 million Japanese travel abroad annually for pleasure or on business. The strong yen encourages them to travel to foreign countries, because overseas travel is often less expensive than domestic travel.

The busiest times for travelling abroad are New Year's vacation, Golden Week, and summer.

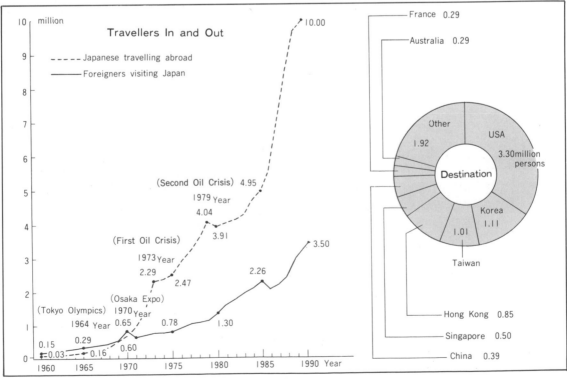

Travellers In and Out

- - - - Japanese travelling abroad
——— Foreigners visiting Japan

(Second Oil Crisis) 4.95
1979 Year
4.04
3.91

(First Oil Crisis)
1973 Year
2.29
2.47

(Osaka Expo)
1970 Year
0.65

(Tokyo Olympics)
1964 Year
0.15   0.29   0.60   0.78   1.30   2.26   3.50
0.03   0.16

10.00

Destination

France 0.29
Australia 0.29
Other 1.92
USA 3.30 million persons
Korea 1.11
Taiwan 1.01
Hong Kong 0.85
Singapore 0.50
China 0.39

Source: Ministry of Justice

MAY　　　　　　5 月

皐<ruby>さ<rt></rt></ruby>
<ruby>つ<rt></rt></ruby>
月<ruby>き<rt></rt></ruby>

Satsuki is the contraction of *Sanaezuki*. *Sanae* means "rice sprouts." It also is "Azalea Month," the month in which *satsuki*, azaleas, are in full bloom.

May in Japan is a month of splendid weather and fresh, green foliage. As there are few rainy days, the weather of this month is called *satukibare**. Many schools have excursions and athletic meetings.

May the 1st is May Day. On this day in many parts of Japan workers hold meetings and festivals.

May the 3rd is Constitution Day, the 4th is a nationwide vacation day, and May the 5th is Children's Day, which makes three consecutive holidays.

Since national holidays are strung together from Greenery Day through Children's Day, this period is called "Golden Week," and people enjoy the holidays taking trips together with friends or families, going clam gathering at low tide or participating in sports. So many people stream out of the city that resorts and roads are packed.

Golden Week, along with the New Year holiday and summer vacation, is a time when people travel to foreign countries. Nowadays, the number of Japanese traveling overseas annually exceeds 10 million (according to a survey in 1990).

Children's Day was formerly called *Tango no Sekku*, a day to celebrate the growth of boys. Today, Children's Day is a day to celebrate the growth of both boy and girl children. Even now, though, families with boys hoist *koinobori***, and display *samurai* dolls and helmets. Also, some people still observe the customs of taking a bath with iris leaves or eating *chimaki* and *kashiwamochi*.

The second Sunday of May is Mother's Day. People give their mothers red carnations and presents to express their gratitude.

May is the season for newly harvested tea. People especially prize green tea made from new tea leaves picked around *Hachijūhachiya**** because of its flavor and fragrance.

* Meaning, "Sunny days of May"

** Carp streamers

*** The eighty-eighth day after the beginning of Spring

6月
JUNE

水無月（みなづき）

1日　衣替え（ころもがえ）
21日ころ　夏至（げし）

　6月は雨の月です。しょうぶ、あじさいなどの花や、雨に洗われた青葉が美しい季節です。気温も上がり蒸し暑い気候となります。

　6月1日は「衣替え」の日です。制服を着る人たちはいっせいに夏服にとりかえます。でも最近は気温が高くなる5月下旬ごろから夏服を着ることも多くなりました。

　この月の雨を「つゆ」といいますが、梅の実の熟すころの雨なので「梅雨（ばいう）」ともいいます。それで梅雨を「つゆ」と読むこともあります。北のオホーツク海高気圧と南の太平洋高気圧が衝突して梅雨前線を作ると、気象庁は「梅雨（つゆ）入り宣言」をします。北から南に長い日本の国ですから「梅雨入り」の時期は地方によってちがいます。ただし北海道に梅雨はありません。長く続く雨は不快ですが、農業用水や生活用水として、梅雨の雨は日本人にはめぐみの雨です。この時期までに稲作農家では田植えをします。梅の実を使って梅酒を作ったり、梅干しをつけたりするのもこのころです。

　1年中で一番昼間の長い日を「夏至（げし）」といいますが、毎年21日ころが夏至です。東京では昼の長さが14時間35分あり、12月の「冬至（とうじ）」にくらべると5時間近く長くなります。

　またこの月は役所や会社ではボーナスの出る月です。ボーナスは年2回、6月と12月に出るところが多いようです。ボーナスや毎月の給料は、最近では給与振込の会社や役所が多くなりました。

漢字のよみかた

<ruby>洗<rt>あら</rt></ruby>われた	<ruby>青葉<rt>あおば</rt></ruby>	<ruby>美<rt>うつく</rt></ruby>しい	<ruby>季節<rt>きせつ</rt></ruby>	<ruby>気温<rt>きおん</rt></ruby>	<ruby>上<rt>あ</rt></ruby>がり
<ruby>蒸<rt>む</rt></ruby>し<ruby>暑<rt>あつ</rt></ruby>い	<ruby>気候<rt>きこう</rt></ruby>	<ruby>１日<rt>ついたち</rt></ruby>	<ruby>衣替<rt>ころもが</rt></ruby>え	<ruby>制服<rt>せいふく</rt></ruby>	<ruby>夏服<rt>なつふく</rt></ruby>
<ruby>最近<rt>さいきん</rt></ruby>	<ruby>下旬<rt>げじゅん</rt></ruby>	5 <ruby>梅<rt>うめ</rt></ruby>の<ruby>実<rt>み</rt></ruby>	<ruby>熟<rt>じゅく</rt></ruby>す	<ruby>梅雨<rt>ばいう</rt></ruby>	オホーツク<ruby>海<rt>かい</rt></ruby>
<ruby>高気圧<rt>こうきあつ</rt></ruby>	<ruby>太平洋<rt>たいへいよう</rt></ruby>	<ruby>衝突<rt>しょうとつ</rt></ruby>	<ruby>梅雨前線<rt>ばいうぜんせん</rt></ruby>	<ruby>作<rt>つく</rt></ruby>る	<ruby>気象庁<rt>きしょうちょう</rt></ruby>
<ruby>梅雨入<rt>つゆい</rt></ruby>り	<ruby>宣言<rt>せんげん</rt></ruby>	<ruby>時期<rt>じき</rt></ruby>	<ruby>地方<rt>ちほう</rt></ruby>	10 <ruby>北海道<rt>ほっかいどう</rt></ruby>	<ruby>続<rt>つづ</rt></ruby>く
<ruby>不快<rt>ふかい</rt></ruby>	<ruby>農業用水<rt>のうぎょうようすい</rt></ruby>	<ruby>生活用水<rt>せいかつようすい</rt></ruby>	<ruby>稲作農家<rt>いなさくのうか</rt></ruby>	<ruby>田植<rt>たう</rt></ruby>え	<ruby>梅酒<rt>うめしゅ</rt></ruby>
<ruby>作<rt>つく</rt></ruby>ったり	<ruby>梅干<rt>うめぼ</rt></ruby>し	<ruby>１年中<rt>いちねんじゅう</rt></ruby>	<ruby>一番<rt>いちばん</rt></ruby>	<ruby>昼間<rt>ひるま</rt></ruby>	<ruby>夏至<rt>げし</rt></ruby>
<ruby>毎年<rt>まいとし</rt></ruby>	15 <ruby>冬至<rt>とうじ</rt></ruby>	<ruby>近<rt>ちか</rt></ruby>く	<ruby>役所<rt>やくしょ</rt></ruby>	<ruby>出<rt>で</rt></ruby>る	<ruby>年2回<rt>ねんにかい</rt></ruby>
<ruby>毎月<rt>まいつき</rt></ruby>	<ruby>給料<rt>きゅうりょう</rt></ruby>	<ruby>給与振込<rt>きゅうよふりこみ</rt></ruby>			

Koromogae
衣替え

Summer is hot and humid, so all who wear uniforms change their clothes to summer-weight uniforms. Many students wear white shirts with short sleeves. Today some of the uniforms of office workers or schools are designed by famous fasion designers, so they are more refined and tasteful than before.

At home, when the weather is sunny and dry, winter clothes are put out to air, and summer clothes replace them in the closet.

Teru teru Bōzu
てるてるぼうず

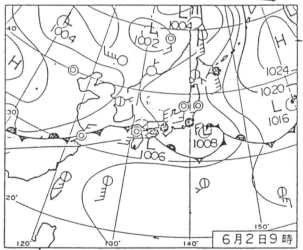

Baiu Zensen   梅雨前線

Baiu zensen (the seasonal rain front) is a stationary front which occurs between the Okhotsk air mass and the Ogasawara air mass. Generally, the rainy season moves up Japan from the west to the northeast. There are two characteristic types of rainy season besides the normal rainy season. One is a "dry" rainy season called *kara-tsuyu*. This happens when the seasonal rain front brings hardly any rain. The *kara-tsuyu* causes bad crops, poor harvest and a shortage of water. The other is a long rainy season called *naga-tsuyu*. It is a long lasting rainy season, which is highly unpleasant.

Teru teru bōzu is a very simple white doll, made of white tissue paper or white cloth. It consists of just a small head and body without hair, nose, mouth, eyes, ears or limbs, and it is hung outside windows or from the eaves to wish for sunny days. Children often hang one when they are hoping for fine weather the next day, and they sing a song of *teru teru bōzu*. This custom was brought to Japan from China many years ago.

Rainfall in Japan　日本の年間雨量

Temperature / Rainfall — Kumamoto

Temperature / Rainfall — Akita

Temperature / Rainfall — Tokyo

Source: Nihon no Sugata
1989 Kokuseisha

Temperature / Rainfall — London

Temperature / Rainfall — Singapore

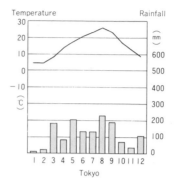

The average annual rainfall in Japan reaches 1600mm. The amount of rain increases in June and September. The rainy season in June brings a lot of rain, but less than typhoon season in September.

In eastern Japan, where the capital city Tokyo is situated, a seasonal wind blows from south to east in summer, and the weather becomes sultry and rainfall is frequent. In winter a seasonal wind blows from the northwest, and the weather is dry and fine with sunshine.

The Bonus System
ボーナス

A bonus was originally a kind of supplementary profit-sharing, but today a bonus is an integral part of a Japanese salaried worker's earnings. Two bonuses are paid, one in summer and one at year's end. The amount of bonus depends on the company and on the length of employment.

Government official's bonuses are paid in June and December. People receive a total bonus of about 5 months' salary every year and they often use it to make a big purchase, or for travelling and so on.

41

The Japanese and Rice 日本人と米

Rice is closely tied to the Japanese diet and culture. Rice was once used for payment of taxes and salaries. Therefore landlords were responsible for making offerings to the gods to ensure an ample rice harvest, and great ritualistic rice festivals were held as official ceremonies in Japan. The importance of rice is decreasing little by little, because Japanese dietary life is changing toward a Western style, which means that people eat more bread, cereal or noodles than they used to. But rice is still Japan's main agricultural product, and rice is still the staple food of the Japanese people.

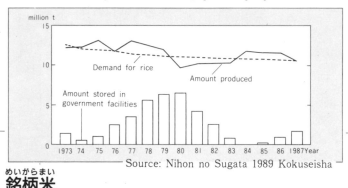

Source: Nihon no Sugata 1989 Kokuseisha

Today mechanical planters and planting tractors are used at rice planting season.

Rice amounts to about 39% of the planted acreage of Japan's agriculture products. In 1990 the rice crop reached about 1 million tons, about 30% of Japan's total agricultural output, down from 52% in 1955. But it isn't that the rice crop has decreased, it's that Japan's output of vegetables, fruits and livestock products has increased.

A kind of rice-planting ceremony to pray for a bountiful harvest of rice is still held today.

めいがらまい
銘柄米
Brands of Rice

Consumers are eager to buy gourmet rice.

Each prefecture competes to produce rice with attractive brand names.

Here are the names of Japanese brands of rice and their main producing districts.

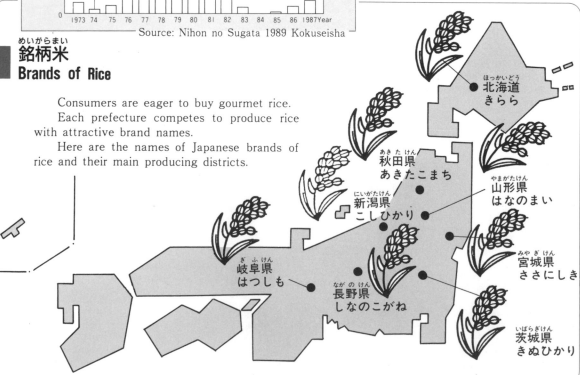

ほっかいどう
北海道
きらら

あきたけん
秋田県
あきたこまち

やまがたけん
山形県
はなのまい

にいがたけん
新潟県
こしひかり

みやぎけん
宮城県
ささにしき

ぎふけん
岐阜県
はつしも

ながのけん
長野県
しなのこがね

いばらぎけん
茨城県
きぬひかり

JUNE 6 月

水無月
みなづき

The characters in *Minazuki* literally mean "no-water-month," but the sound itself is just as the old way of reading the characters 「水月」—"Water Month." Anyway, *Minazuki* means "the month of water." Around this time of year, farmers hope for abundant rain for the rice paddies.

June is the month for rain. It is the season when flowers such as iris and hydrangea are beautiful with their young, green leaves glistening in the rain. The temperature is rising, and the air is becoming humid.

June 1st is "change of dress day." On this day all who wear uniforms change to summer styles. But in the past few years many people have begun wearing their summer uniforms at the end of May, when the weather is getting hot.

We call the rain of this month *tsuyu*, and because it comes at the same time when plums are ripening, we also call this rain *baiu* and read the Chinese characters as *tsuyu**. When the high pressure system over the Okhotsk Sea to the north collides with the high pressure of the Pacific Ocean to the south to form a seasonal rain front, the Meteorological Agency announces the official beginning of the rainy season. Japan is a country covering a long distance from north to south, so the opening of the rainy season varies from location to location. However, there is no rainy season in Hokkaido.

Although this long-lasting rain is unpleasant, rain is important as water for agriculture and daily life, so the rain of *tsuyu* is a rain of blessing for the Japanese people. By this time, farmers have done rice planting. Families use the ripened plums to make plum brandy or pickled plums.

The day of the year when daylight is longest is called *Geshi*, and every year the Summer Solstice is around the 21st. In Tokyo this day is 14 hours and 35 minutes long, five hours longer than the Winter Solstice in December.

June is the month when public officials and company employees get bonuses. Bonuses are given out twice a year, usually in June and December. Nowadays many companies and government offices pay monthly salaries and bonuses by bank account transfer.

*   *Tsuyu* and *baiu* are two readings for the combination of two *kanji* which mean
    "plum" and "rain"

7月
JULY

文月（ふみづき）

7日　七夕（たなばた）

　　7月になると各地で「海開き」「山開き」が行われ、海水浴、夏山登山シーズンが始まります。

　　7月7日は「七夕（たなばた）」です。伝説によると、はたおり姫の「織女星（しょくじょせい）」と恋人の牛飼いの「牽牛星（けんぎゅうせい）」が、1年にたった一度天の川で会う日だといわれています。
5　この日には子供たちはたんざくに願いごとを書いて、ささ竹につるします。おり紙でくさりや天の川も作ってかざります。

　　中旬をすぎて梅雨前線が北上するか消えると、気象庁が「梅雨明け宣言」を出します。梅雨が明けると、いよいよ本格的な夏の始まりです。最高気温が30度をこえる真夏日も多く、明け方の最低気温が25度以下にならない熱帯夜が続
10　きます。このころの土用の丑（うし）の日には夏バテをしないように、うなぎのかば焼きを食べる風習があり、うなぎの需要がふえる時です。

　　1日から15日の間に日頃お世話になった人々におくり物をする習慣があります。これを「お中元」といって、デパートや商店街は「中元大売り出し」でにぎわいます。

15　また、中旬から8月上旬までの間に暑中見舞いのはがきを出して、元気に暮らしているかをどうかをたずねます。

　　20日ごろ学校では1学期が終わって終業式をします。4月に小学校に入った子供たちは、はじめて通知表をもらいます。そして約40日間の夏休みが始まります。夏休みには学校から宿題が出されますが、子供たちは友だちや家族といっ
20　しょに野外活動や合宿、旅行に出かけます。

　　大学や高校の受験生にとっては、夏休みは集中して受験勉強をする時です。予備校や塾では夏期講習が開かれ、朝から夜まで多くの受験生たちが出席します。

漢字のよみかた

各地　海開き　山開き　行われ　海水浴　夏山登山

始まります　7日　七夕　伝説　はたおり姫　織女星

恋人　牛飼い　牽牛星　一度　天の川　会う

5　子供たち　願いごと　ささ竹　おり紙　作って　中旬

梅雨前線　北上する　消える　気象庁　梅雨明け　宣言

出します　明ける　本格的な　最高気温　真夏日　明け方

最低　以下　熱帯夜　続きます　10　土用　丑の日

かば焼き　風習　需要　日頃　お世話　おくり物

習慣　お中元　商店街　中元大売り出し　15　上旬

暑中見舞い　暮らして　20日　1学期　終わって　終業式

入った　通知表　約40日間　宿題　友だち　家族

20　野外活動　合宿　旅行　出かけます　受験生　集中して

受験勉強　予備校　塾　夏期講習　開かれ　出席します

Tanabata
七 夕

Originally part of the preparation for the *Bon* Festival, *Tanabata* combines many forkloric traditions. A *hata* (or *bata*) is a loom, on which chosen young girls used to weave cloth for the gods; setting looms on platforms or shelves (*tana* in Japanese) at the river side. Later, the star festival of Chinese origin was combined with these traditions in today's *Tanabata* Festival. Children write wishes on *tanzaku* (strips of paper) in five colors, mainly praying for success in their studies.

Kindergarteners and primary schoolchildren decorate bamboo branches and celebrate the festival in the classroom with drinks and sweets. Some kindergartens have a dance and song festival.

Children bring home their decorations of bamboo branches and eat special food.

In some areas today, *Tanabata* has become an elaborate tourist attraction. Gigantic bamboo poles, decorated with colorful vinyl and plastic factory-made ornaments — balls, strips and clusters — are set up on the streets in shopping areas.

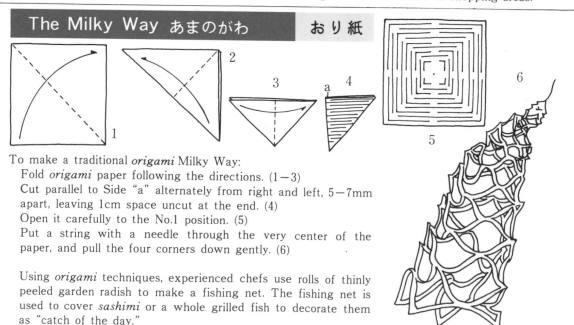

The Milky Way あまのがわ おり紙

To make a traditional *origami* Milky Way:
Fold *origami* paper following the directions. (1—3)
Cut parallel to Side "a" alternately from right and left, 5—7mm apart, leaving 1cm space uncut at the end. (4)
Open it carefully to the No.1 position. (5)
Put a string with a needle through the very center of the paper, and pull the four corners down gently. (6)

Using *origami* techniques, experienced chefs use rolls of thinly peeled garden radish to make a fishing net. The fishing net is used to cover *sashimi* or a whole grilled fish to decorate them as "catch of the day."

O-chūgen
お中元

Twice a year, at the beginning of July and December, come the big seasons for gift-exchanging in Japan. In summer it is called *o-chūgen*. This originated in the custom that relatives got together in their hometown, bringing food to honor their ancestors. Later, instead of gathering, they started just sending gifts to each other. Just as in earlier times, food items such as drinks, fruits, summer cakes and sweets, dried noodles and canned food are popular *o-chūgen* gifts. Tickets for beer and ice cream are also sold as summer gifts.

Shochū Mimai 暑中見舞い

「暑中御見舞い申し上げます」 *Shochū omimai mōshiagemasu* "How are you getting along in this heat?" is a set formula for midsummer greeting cards sent out before *Risshū*, around the 6th of August, which the lunar calendar calls the beginning of autumn. Sending cards after *Risshū* 「残暑」 *Zansho* meaning "the lingering summer heat" is used instead of 「暑中」.

At the beginning of June, the post office starts to sell special post cards for midsummer greetings. Summer greeting cards which have a nickname of "*Kamo* Mail" — a compound noun of "*kamome*" (sea gull) and "mail," and a pun on the English phrase, "Come on, Mail!" — have lot numbers and a special summer design for the printed stamp on the front.

Ushi no Hi
うしの日

Eating eel for vigor during *doyō*, the hottest summer days, is a custom handed down from the Edo Period (1603-1867). On *Ushi no Hi* (the Day of the Cow) eels are believed to taste especially appetizing, and the aroma of broiled eel, dipped in special soy-*mirin* sauce, wafts out from restaurants and roadside stands.

Today most eels are raised commercially in Japan or imported from Taiwan and other countries.

Special Summer Classes
移動教室

During summer vacation, schoolchildren enjoy special classes, staying for several days at mountain or beach cottages owned by the school or local government. The program is called "*idō kyōshitsu*" (moved-afar classroom). Children share group-life experiences together — studying, playing, singing, cooking, and so on.

Some attend specialized training camps sponsored by school clubs. Some choose from a variety of programs offered by private organizations. Now it is in fashion for high school students to go overseas to stay with local families.

Extra Summer School
夏期講習

Examination candidates study at cram schools — called "*juku*" for younger pupils, and "*yobikō*" for high school students — to memorize important points of subjects and learn techniques to win the hectic competition of entrance exams. In spite of the summer heat, they study hard now and at special wintertime courses immediately prior to the exam. Some students tie a piece of cloth around their head to show a firm resolution to challenge and win.

夏の味、夏の野山
Summer Food, Flora and Fauna

すずらん	Lily of the valley
ほおずき	Ground cherry
くちなし	Gardenia
すいれん	Water lily
あじさい	Hydrangea
しょうぶ	Iris
朝顔	Morning-glory
ひまわり	Sunflower
ほうせんか	Balsam
ゆり	Lily
きょうちくとう	Sweet oleander
さるすべり	Crape myrtle
ほたる	Firefly
かぶと虫	Beetle
きんぎょ	Goldfish

初がつお	The first bonito on the market
あゆ	Sweetfish
きす	Sillago, a Japanese silver whiting
うなぎ	Eel
新茶	The first-picked tea of the season
さくらんぼ	Cherries
びわ	Loquat, a Japanese medlar
すいか	Watermelon
とうもろこし	Corn
えだまめ	Green soybeans
そうめん	Thin noodles, a kind of Japanese vermicelli, served with cold dip sauce with soy flavor.
むぎ茶	Toasted barley tea
ひややっこ	Chilled bean curd, *tōfu*, cut in cubes served with soy sauce.

JULY 7 月

文 ふ
み
月 づ
き

July is called *Fumizuki*, written with the characters for "literature" or "book" and "month."
The origin of the name goes back to several sources. At the end of the Heian Era, for example, July was the month to fashion letters in formal language or write poems in Chinese for the *Tanabata* Festival, opening books to refer.

When July comes, the swimming and summer-mountaineering seasons begin, and ceremonies are held in various places to mark "the opening of the sea to swimmers" and "the opening of the mountains to climbers."

July 7th is *Tanabata*.*   According to legend, this is the one day in the year when two lovers, the weaver star *Vega* and the shepherd star *Altair*, meet in the Milky Way. On this day, children write wishes and hang them on bamboo branches, and decorate the branches with paper chains and a Milky Way made of *origami*.

After midmonth, when the seasonal rain front heads north or disappears, the Meteorological Agency officially announces the end of the rainy season. When the rainy season is over, the real summer finally begins. There are many "high summer days" when the highest temperature reaches 30 degrees, and "tropical nights" continue with early-morning low temperatures never dipping below 25. To counteract the energy-draining effect of the summer heat, even today there is a custom of eating broiled eel on the "Day of the Cow" during the hottest period, and on that day the demand for eel increases sharply at shops and restaurants.

From the 1st to the 15th, people customarily send gifts to those who have been especially kind to them. This is called *o-chūgen*, and department stores and shopping centers are thronged with shoppers at special *o-chūgen* sales.

From mid-month through the first part of August, people send "midsummer greeting cards" to inquire after each other's health during the hot summer days.

Around the 20th, the first school term ends with a term closing ceremony. Children who started elementary school in April receive their first report cards. And a 40-day summer vacation begins. Although students bring home summer assignments from school, still there is time for outdoor activities, going to camp, and trips with their friends and family.

For those who will soon take university and high school entrance examinations, summer vacation is the time to study intensively. Cram schools and *juku* provide summer courses, and many students attend from early in the morning until late at night.

* Star Festival; Festival of the Weaver

8月
AUGUST

葉
月
_{はづき}

6日　広島原爆記念日
　　　_{ひろしまげんばくきねんび}
9日　長崎原爆記念日
　　　_{ながさきげんばくきねんび}
15日　終戦記念日
　　　_{しゅうせんきねんび}

　　8月初めは太平洋高気圧の勢いが強いので、全国的に晴天が続き、各地で最高気温を記録することがあります。

　　6日は広島、9日は長崎の「原爆記念日」です。また、15日は「終戦記念日」で、各地で平和を祈る集会や行事が行われます。

5　　8月は「お盆」の月です。13日から15日のお盆は仏教の行事で、なくなった先祖の霊を家に迎える日です。門の前で迎え火をたいたり、仏だんの前に野菜をそなえたりしてお盆の準備をします。盆踊りや花火大会もあちらこちらでさかんに行われます。16日には「送り火」をたいて先祖の霊を見送ります。京都の「大文字」の送り火は特に有名です。また、この日に「とうろう流し」をして先祖を見送る地方もあります。

10　　ほとんどの会社や商店はこのころをお盆休みにしています。2、3日から10日ぐらいのお盆休みを利用して、帰省したり、海や山に遊びに行ったりします。そのため駅や空港にはおみやげをたくさん持った人たちがみられ、長距離列車や飛行機などの交通機関が大混雑します。幹線道路には数十キロの車の列ができることもよくあります。

15　　8月には夏の「全国高校野球選手権大会」が開かれます。日本全国から地区予選を勝ち抜いたチームが兵庫県の甲子園球場に集まって、日本一を競います。各県代表が出場しているので、人々は自分の出身県や地元のチームを応援します。

20　　高校野球が終わると8月も終わりに近づき、海や山へ出かける人も少なくなります。

50

漢字のよみかた

初め (はじめ)	太平洋 (たいへいよう)	高気圧 (こうきあつ)	勢い (いきお)	強い (つよ)	全国的 (ぜんこくてき)
晴天 (せいてん)	続き (つづ)	各地 (かくち)	最高気温 (さいこうきおん)	記録する (きろく)	6日 (むいか)
広島 (ひろしま)	9日 (ここのか)	長崎 (ながさき)	原爆記念日 (げんばくきねんび)	終戦記念日 (しゅうせんきねんび)	平和 (へいわ)
祈る (いの)	集会 (しゅうかい)	行事 (ぎょうじ)	行われます (おこな)	⁵お盆 (ぼん)	仏教 (ぶっきょう)
先祖 (せんぞ)	霊 (れい)	迎える (むか)	迎え火 (むか び)	仏だん (ぶつ)	野菜 (やさい)
準備 (じゅんび)	盆踊り (ぼんおど)	花火大会 (はなびたいかい)	送り火 (おく び)	見送ります (みおく)	大文字 (だいもんじ)
特に (とく)	有名 (ゆうめい)	とうろう流し (なが)	¹⁰地方 (ちほう)	商店 (しょうてん)	お盆休み (ぼんやす)
2、3日 (に さんにち)	10日 (とおか)	利用して (りよう)	帰省したり (きせい)	遊び (あそ)	空港 (くうこう)
長距離列車 (ちょうきょりれっしゃ)	飛行機 (ひこうき)	交通機関 (こうつうきかん)	大混雑します (だいこんざつ)	幹線道路 (かんせんどうろ)	数十キロ (すうじっ)
列 (れつ)	¹⁵全国高校野球選手権大会 (ぜんこくこうこうやきゅうせんしゅけんたいかい)	開かれます (ひら)	日本全国 (にほんぜんこく)	地区予選 (ちくよせん)	
勝ち抜いた (か ぬ)	兵庫県 (ひょうごけん)	甲子園球場 (こうしえんきゅうじょう)	集まって (あつ)	日本一 (にほんいち)	競います (きそ)
各県代表 (かくけんだいひょう)	出場して (しゅつじょう)	自分 (じぶん)	出身県 (しゅっしんけん)	地元 (じもと)	応援します (おうえん)
²⁰終わる (お)	近づき (ちか)	出かける (で)			

Tōrō Nagashi
とうろう流し

Another form of *okuribi* is *tōrō nagashi*, floating paper lanterns. These paper lanterns have lighted candles inside, and people float them on a river to guide their ancestors' souls down the river and off to the sea. There are different ways to practice *tōrō nagashi*, according to each locale.

O-bon お盆

Most Japanese celebrate *O-bon*, from August 13th to 15th. According to Buddhist tradition, the souls of one's ancestors return to this world during this time of year. To guide the souls to their home, a "horse" is made of summer vegetables, and a fire called *mukaebi* is lit and placed in front of the gate at each household. During *O-bon* a Buddhist monk pays a visit to each temple member's house to chant a sutra, which is a part of the Buddhist religious service. *Okuribi* is a fire lit on August 16th to send the souls off to the world of the dead.

Bon Odori 盆おどり

Bon odori, folk dancing, is held in many communities all over the country during *O-bon* season. Men and women, young and old, are clad in *yukata* (summer cotton *kimono*), and dance to the music in a circle around the *yagura* (a standing stage). Each locale has its own traditional style of *bon odori*.

Daimonji
大文字

People light huge send-off fires on five mountains surrounding the city of Kyoto. Among these the one called *"Daimonji,"* which has the shape of the Chinese character 大 (pronounced as "dai" and meaning "large."), is the most famous. At eight o'clock in the evening of August 16th, fires are set on Mt. Nyoigatake, and a huge Chinese character "dai" appears on the dark slope of the mountain. Five other send-off fires on four mountains are lit one by one to form different patterns.

Homecoming   帰　省

Many people who work in large cities such as Tokyo and Osaka come from hometowns in other parts of Japan. New Year's *(O-shogatsu)* and *O-bon* have been two important occasions for Japanese families to get together; thus, long lines of cars, sometimes up to 50-60 kilometers, are formed on major freeways and highways. Airports and train stations are equally crowded.

O-bon Holidays
お盆休み

Many shops and restaurants as well as offices are closed during *O-bon*. Office districts in Tokyo, usually crowded with businessmen in a hurry, become deserted during this time. Many people return to their hometowns; others go to resort areas or travel overseas.

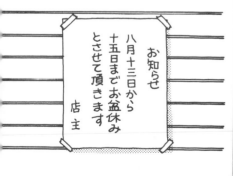

お知らせ

八月十三日から
十五日までお盆休み
とさせて頂きます

店主

Anniversaries of the Atomic Bombing　原爆記念日

At the end of World War II, two atomic bombs were dropped over the cities of Hiroshima and Nagasaki by the American military forces. These were the first and only cases in the history of mankind that atomic bombs were used. It is established that 90,000 −120,000 people died in or within four months of the explosion at Hiroshima; at Nagasaki, it was 60,000−70,000. Thousands more who survived the blasts have died from its effects, or are still suffering today from radiation poisoning and other injuries.

Determined that such tragedy will never be repeated, many people gather on August 6th, 9th and 15th at Atomic Bomb Memorial Parks in Hiroshima and Nagasaki.

Peace Marches
平和行進

Rallies and demonstration marches for world peace are held on the anniversary of the end of the World War II.

The All-Japan High School Baseball Tournament　全国高校野球 選手権大会

The All-Japan High School Baseball Tournament was first held in 1915 in Osaka. Except during the war years from 1942 to 1946, the tournament has been held every year and attracts many baseball fans throughout the country. In 1915, only 73 high schools (then 5-year middle schools) participated. The number of participating schools has steadily increased and in 1991, 4,046 schools competed in the tournament.

AUGUST 8 月

葉は
づ
月き

Hazuki means "Leaf Month."
An old legend tells that the leaves of the great laurel tree in the moon turn bright yellow around this time of year, and this makes the moonlight brighter.

Since the Pacific Ocean high pressure system is very strong in the beginning of August, there are hot, sunny days with record-high temperatures throughout the country.

The 6th and the 9th are the anniversaries of the atomic bombings of Hiroshima and Nagasaki. Then, the 15th is the anniversary of the end of World War II, and all over Japan rallies and events are held to pray for peace.

August is the month for *O-bon*. The 13th to the 15th is the Buddhist "Festival of the Dead," and these are the days to welcome home the souls of departed ancestors. Families prepare for *O-bon* by lighting a welcome fire outside the gate and making decorations out of vegetables. *O-bon* dances and fireworks displays are held in many places. On the 16th, people light send-off fires and see the souls off. In Kyoto, the huge send-off fire called *Daimonji* is especially famous. Also, there are localities where the spirits are sent off with floating paper lanterns.

Most companies and stores take *O-bon* holidays at this time of year. Making use of *O-bon* holidays time of two or three or even ten days, people travel to their hometowns or go to the beach or the mountains. At train stations and airports you can see many people toting souvenir gifts, and long-distance trains and airplanes are packed. On the highways, often cars are backed up for a few to 50-60 kilometers.

The summer All-Japan High School Baseball Tournament is held in August. From all over Japan, the district champions gather at Koshien Stadium in Hyogo Prefecture and compete to be No.1 in Japan. Since each prefecture is represented in the tournament, people cheer their local team or the team from their old hometown.

When the high school baseball tournament is over, the summer too is over, and so is the season for mountain and beach-going.

日本のまつり

Japanese Festivals

●1月
群馬（ぐんま）	だるま市（いち） 1/6-7
大阪（おおさか）	今宮十日戒（いまみやとうかえびす） 1/10
長野（ながの）	野沢温泉道祖神火まつり（のざわおんせんどうそじんひ） 1/15
愛知（あいち）	国府宮裸まつり（こうのみやはだか） 旧暦（きゅうれき）1/13

●2月
北海道（ほっかいどう）	札幌雪まつり（さっぽろゆき） 2/1-5
千葉（ちば）	成田山節分会（なりたさんせつぶんえ） 2/3
奈良（なら）	春日大社万灯会（かすがたいしゃまんとうえ） 2/3 8/15
岡山（おかやま）	西大寺裸まつり（さいだいじはだか） 2月（だい）第3土曜日（どようび）

●3月
| 熊本（くまもと） | 阿蘇神社火振りまつり（あそじんじゃひふ） 3月中旬、下旬申の日（ちゅうじゅん、げじゅんさる ひ） |
| 鳥取（とっとり） | 流しびな（なが） 旧暦（きゅうれき）3/3 |

●4月
高知（こうち）	どろんこまつり 4月第1日曜をはさむ3日間（だいいちにちようかかん）
新潟（にいがた）	新潟チューリップまつり 4/10-5/15
岐阜（ぎふ）	高山まつり（たかやま） 春4/14-15・秋10/9-10（はるあき）
福井（ふくい）	仏の舞（ほとけまい） 4/18隔年（かくねん）
山口（やまぐち）	下関先帝祭（しものせきせんていさい） 4/23-25

●5月
静岡（しずおか）	浜松まつり（はままつ） 5/3-5
東京（とうきょう）	三社まつり（さんじゃ） 5月第3日曜日を最終日とする4日間（だいさんにちようびさいしゅうびよっかかん）
栃木（とちぎ）	東照宮千人武者行列（とうしょうぐうせんにんむしゃぎょうれつ） 5/18
兵庫（ひょうご）	楠公まつり（なんこう） 5/24-26
沖縄（おきなわ）	ハーリー競漕（きょうそう） 旧暦（きゅうれき）5/4

●6月
茨城（いばらぎ）	潮来あやめまつり（いたこ） 6/1-30
石川（いしかわ）	加賀百万石まつり（かがひゃくまんごく） 6/12-14
岩手（いわて）	チャグチャグ馬コ（うま） 6/15
広島（ひろしま）	厳島神社管弦祭（いつくしまじんじゃかんげんさい） 旧暦（きゅうれき）6/17

青森ねぶた（青森）

時代まつり（京都）

今宮十日戒（大阪）

鷺舞（島根）

長崎くんち（長崎）

阿波踊（徳島）

札幌雪まつり（北海道）

チャグチャグ馬コ（岩手）

秋田竿灯（秋田）

仙台七夕まつり（宮城）

だるま市（群馬）

浜松まつり（静岡）

那智の火まつり（和歌山）

●7月
宮城	仙台七夕まつり	7/6-7
山形	花笠まつり	7/6-8
福岡	博多祇園山笠	7/13-15
和歌山	那智の火まつり	7/14
島根	鷺舞	7/20-21

●8月
青森	青森ねぶた	8/2-7
秋田	秋田竿灯	8/5-7
徳島	阿波踊り	8/12-15
山梨	吉田の火まつり	8/26

●9月
富山	越中おわら風の盆	9/1-3
福島	会津白虎まつり	9/22-24

●10月
長崎	長崎くんち	10/7-9
香川	金刀比羅宮大祭	10/9-11
大分	ケベスまつり	10/14
京都	時代まつり	10/15
愛媛	西条まつり	10/15-16
三重	お伊勢大祭	10/15-17
滋賀	彦根お城まつり	10月中旬
宮崎	宮崎神社大祭	10月最終土・日曜日-11/3

●11月
佐賀	唐津くんち	11/2-4
神奈川	箱根大名行列	11/3
鹿児島	おはらまつり	11/3

●12月
| 埼玉 | 秩父夜まつり | 12/2-3 |

9月
SEPTEMBER

長月（ながつき）

1日　防災の日（ぼうさい ひ）
15日　敬老の日（けいろう ひ）
23日ころ　秋分の日（しゅうぶん ひ）

　　長い夏休みが終わり、ほとんどの学校では9月から2学期が始まります。
　　2学期は学年の真ん中の学期にあたり、運動会や学園祭などいろいろ行事が多い時期です。
　　9月1日は「防災の日」です。1923年9月1日の関東大震災の惨事をくりかえさないために、全国の学校、役所、会社、地域などで避難訓練が行われます。
　　また、9月は台風の多い月です。台風の影響で木がたおれたり、農作物に被害が出たり、洪水が起ったりします。大型台風が日本に近づいて来ると、テレビやラジオで夜遅くまで台風の進路、風速、降水量など台風情報を放送します。
　　9月の前半はまだ夏の太平洋高気圧が強く、残暑がきびしいですが、中旬をすぎるころから朝晩の気温が下がって、秋らしくなってきます。日本では秋の夜長にこおろぎ、きりぎりすなど美しい声で鳴く虫の音を音楽のように楽しんでいます。
　　またこのころの満月を「中秋の名月（ちゅうしゅう めいげつ）」といい、昔から日本人は1年中で一番美しい月として「お月見」を楽しんできました。お月見は月見だんご、すすき、ぶどうやくりなど季節のくだものをそなえて月を観賞する行事です。最近では高層ビルやマンションが多くなったので月を見ることができなくなったり、日常生活がいそがしくなって、お月見をする人は少なくなりました。
　　15日は「敬老の日」です。お年寄りに感謝する日です。
　　23日ごろは「秋分の日」です。秋分の日を中心として秋のお彼岸には春と同じようにお墓参りをします。このころからしだいに、夜が長くなります。

漢字のよみかた

終(お)わり	2学期(にがっき)	始(はじ)まります	真(ま)ん中(なか)	運動会(うんどうかい)	学園祭(がくえんさい)
行事(ぎょうじ)	時期(じき)	1日(ついたち)	防災(ぼうさい)の日(ひ)	関東大震災(かんとうだいしんさい)	惨事(さんじ)
5 全国(ぜんこく)	役所(やくしょ)	地域(ちいき)	避難訓練(ひなんくんれん)	行(おこな)われます	台風(たいふう)
影響(えいきょう)	農作物(のうさくぶつ)	被害(ひがい)	洪水(こうずい)	起(おこ)ったり	大型台風(おおがたたいふう)
近(ちか)づいて	来(く)る	夜遅(よるおそ)く	進路(しんろ)	風速(ふうそく)	降水量(こうすいりょう)
台風情報(たいふうじょうほう)	放送(ほうそう)	前半(ぜんはん)	太平洋(たいへいよう)	高気圧(こうきあつ)	強(つよ)く
残暑(ざんしょ)	中旬(ちゅうじゅん)	10 朝晩(あさばん)	気温(きおん)	下(さ)がって	夜長(よなが)
美(うつく)しい	声(こえ)	鳴(な)く	虫(むし)の音(ね)	音楽(おんがく)	楽(たの)しんで
満月(まんげつ)	中秋(ちゅうしゅう)の名月(めいげつ)	昔(むかし)	1年中(いちねんじゅう)	一番(いちばん)	お月見(つきみ)
15 季節(きせつ)	観賞(かんしょう)する	行事(ぎょうじ)	最近(さいきん)	高層(こうそう)ビル	日常生活(にちじょうせいかつ)
敬老(けいろう)の日(ひ)	お年寄(としよ)り	感謝(かんしゃ)する	秋分(しゅうぶん)の日(ひ)	中心(ちゅうしん)	お彼岸(ひがん)
同(おな)じ	20 お墓参(はかまい)り	夜(よる)			

Emergency Bag
非常持ち出し袋

Now each home is advised to have an emergency bag, which you can buy at supermarkets or department stores.

The emergency bag is marked "To Be Taken Out In Case Of Emergency." It includes: ⇨

Typhoon
台 風

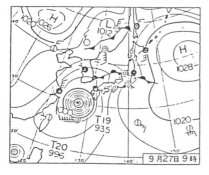

Typical weather chart when a typhoon is approaching;

Disaster Prevention Day　　防災の日

On September 1, 1923, a big earthquake with magnitude 7.9.～8.2 hit the Kanto area. According to the record, 99,331 were killed, 43,476 missing, 103,733 injured. 128,266 houses were ruined, 126,233 half-ruined, 447,128 burnt.

To prevent such tragedy, September 1st was designated to be Disaster Prevention Day. On this day, earthquake and fire drills are held all over the country. Children and adults alike put on helmets, and drill under the direction of firefighters.

Now many people live and work in the congested cities and drills are held at highrise buildings using helicopters.

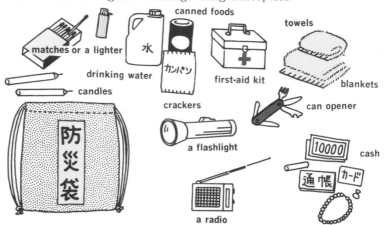

A typhoon is a kind of low pressure system that forms and develops in the southern seas, and attacks the Philippines, China, Japan, etc. About 28 typhoons form annually, but only a few of them, perhaps 4, land at Japan. The earliest typhoon to attack Japan was in May, and the latest one recorded was in December, but most of them come in August and September.

The recent Tyhoon #19 of 1991 caused heavy losses to agriculture, forestry and fishery. Apples and oranges were especially hard hit, the worst in history. Total damage was estimated at 390 billion yen.

When a typhoon is coming near the Japanese Archipelago, people watch the TV weather forecast carefully, and prepare to avoid damage.

Respect for the Aged Day was instituted in 1966 as a national holiday because it was recognized that the number of the aged would increase rapidly in the future and the whole nation should have a clear awareness of it. On September 15th, people visit their parents, grandparents and/or aged acquaintances to show respect for the aged.

長寿の祝い
Celebration of Longevity

In Japan, as in China, people traditionally celebrate their longevity as well as their health on their 60th and 70th birthdays. And the Japanese have even more celebrations for ages 77, 88 and 99, because double numbers are favored, with a saying that luck also doubles in those years.

還暦 *Kanreki*
60th Birthday : 還：return, 暦：calendar
Returning to the same *eto* year of one's birth after living through the 60-year cycle.

古希 *Koki*
70th Birthday : 古：the olden times, 稀：rare
Man rarely lived until the age of 70 in the olden times.

喜寿 *Kiju*
77th Birthday : 喜 ➡ 㐂 ➡ 七十七
The character "joy(喜)", when written in cursive style, resembles the characters for seventy-seven. So the celebration of the 77th birthday is called *Kiju*, Joyful Celebration.

傘寿 *Sanju*
80th Birthday : 傘 ➡ 仐 ➡ 八十
The characters "eighty," when written in cursive style, resembles the character "umbrella (傘)." So the celebration of the 80th birthday is called *Sanju*, Umbrella Celebration.

米寿 *Beiju*
88th Birthday : 米 ➡ 八十八
The characters "eighty-eight," when put together resembles the characer "rice (米)." So the celebration of the 88th birthday is called *Beiju*, Rice Celebration.

卒寿 *Sotsuju*
90th Birthday : 卒 ➡ 卆 ➡ 九十
The character "finish"(卒), when written in simplified form, resembles the characters "ninety". So the celebration of the 90th birthday is called *Sotsuju*, Finishing Celebration.

白寿 *Hakuju*
99th Birthday : 百 ― ― = 白
When one stroke is taken away from the character "one hundred (百)," it becomes "white (白)." So the celebration of the 99th birthday is called *Hakuju*, White Celebration.

Aging Society 高齢化社会

●The Ratio of the Aged (65 and up) to the Entire Population

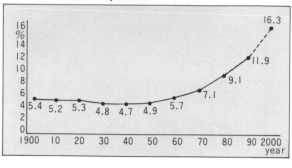

Recently the life expectancy of the Japanese people has extended, and the population of the aged has increased. In 1935 the ratio of the aged to the entire population was 4.7%, becoming 5.3% in 1955. By 1991 it more than doubled to 12.5%.

And it will continue to rise as the birth rate is decreasing. At the end of the 20th Century it will be 15.6%, and 20% in the first half of the next century.

●The Average Life Expectancy of the Japanese

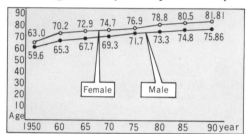

Source : Statistic Bureau of the Management and Coordination Agency

Moon Viewing お月見

The full moon in the clear autumn sky is beautiful, especially after the long summer heat.

In the ancient Chinese court, moon viewing was one of the major celebrations.

It was held on the night of the full moon in the middle of autumn. This custom was introduced to Japan in the beginning of the 10th Century, and the first official moon viewing (*o-tsukimi*) was held on August 15th, 909, of the lunar calendar. Since then not only the court but ordinary people have enjoyed moon viewing.

For moon viewing, dumplings, made round in the shape of the moon, are offered to the moon. Also people would offer flowers like *obana* (*susuki*), *ominaeshi* or *hagi* together with fruits of the season.

Looking at the patterns made by craters on the surface of the moon, the Japanese believed they could see the form of a rabbit making rice cakes.

長月 _{ながつき}

Nagatsuki means a "Long Month" or "Long Moon." Many poets appreciated the beautiful moon in the sky during the long autumn night.

The long summer vacation is over, and at most schools the second term begins in September.

Second term is the middle period of the school year, so it is the time for many events such as athletic meeting and campus festivals.

The 1st is Disaster Prevention Day. In the hope that a disaster like the Great Kanto Earthquake of Sept. 1st. 1923, will not be repeated, earthquake and fire drills are held in schools, municipal offices, companies and communities all over the country.

September is also the month for typhoons. In a typhoon trees crash to the ground, crops are ruined, and floodwaters rise. When a big typhoon is coming close to Japan, the television and radio broadcast information about its course, wind velocity and rainfall until late at night.

During the first half of September, when the Pacific Ocean high pressure system prevails, the late summer heat is strong; but after mid-month, the temperature drops mornings and evenings, and autumn is in the air. In Japan people enjoy the music of crickets and other insects singing through the long autumn nights.

The full moon at this time of year is called *Chūshū no Meigetsu**, and since olden times the Japanese people have enjoyed *o-tsukimi*, viewing the most beautiful moon of the year. For *o-tsukimi* people would offer *tsukimi* dumplings, Japanese pampas grass, grapes, chestnuts and other fruits of the season in appreciation of the moon. Now that there are more highrise office and apartment buildings, people cannot see the moon, and lifestyles have become busy, so very few people practice moon-viewing.

September 15th is Respect for the Aged Day. This is a day to express gratitude to elderly people.

September 23rd is the Autumnal Equinox. During the week around the Equinox Day, the same as in the spring, people visit the graves of their ancestors. With this day as the dividing point, the nights are getting longer.

* Beautiful moon of mid-autumn

10月
OCTOBER

神無月（かんなづき）

1日 衣替え（ころもがえ）
10日 体育の日（たいいくのひ）

　10月1日は「衣替え」の日です。この日から夏の制服が冬服にかわります。

　また、1日から「赤い羽根共同募金」が始まります。電車の駅などで、有志の人たちや学生が募金活動をします。募金箱にお金を入れると、胸に赤い羽根をつけてくれます。

5　10月10日は「体育の日」です。1964年10月10日に「東京オリンピック」の開会式がありました。それを記念してスポーツを楽しむ日になりました。この日を中心に幼稚園や学校、町内会や会社では運動会を開きます。家族はお弁当を持って参加します。

　下旬には競馬の秋の天皇賞レースやプロ野球の日本シリーズ、秋の国民体育
10　大会があります。

　10月は結婚式が多い月です。大安などの吉日に、ホテルや結婚式場、神社、教会などでつぎつぎに結婚式があげられます。結婚式のスタイルは宗教とはほとんど関係ありません。式の後、披露宴が行われますが、花よめだけでなく、花むこもお色直しをするなど年々はなやかになっています。

15　10月は暑くもなく寒くもなく、おだやかな気候で、さわやかな秋晴れが続きます。そのため、この時期は行楽のシーズンでもあります。家族連れで果樹園に出かけ、なしもぎやりんご狩りを楽しみます。野山にはいろいろな木の実がなります。幼稚園児や小学生はくりひろいやいもほりに出かけます。都会のやおやの店先にもまつたけ、なし、くり、かきなどの秋の野菜や果物がならび、
20　新米も出始めます。さば、いわし、さんまなどの魚もおいしい時期です。

漢字のよみかた

ついたち 1日	ころもが 衣替え	せいふく 制服	ふゆふく 冬服	あかはね 赤い羽根	きょうどうぼきん 共同募金
はじ 始まります	ゆうし 有志	ぼきんかつどう 募金活動	ぼきんばこ 募金箱	い 入れる	むね 胸
5　とうか 10日	たいいくひ 体育の日	かいかいしき 開会式	きねん 記念して	たの 楽しむ	ちゅうしん 中心
ようちえん 幼稚園	ちょうないかい 町内会	うんどうかい 運動会	ひら 開きます	かぞく 家族	べんとう お弁当
さんか 参加します	げじゅん 下旬	けいば 競馬	てんのうしょう 天皇賞	プロ野球 プロ野球	こくみんたいいくたいかい 国民体育大会
10　けっこんしき 結婚式	たいあん 大安	きちじつ 吉日	けっこんしきじょう 結婚式場	じんじゃ 神社	きょうかい 教会
しゅうきょう 宗教	かんけい 関係	しき 式	あと 後	ひろうえん 披露宴	おこな 行われます
いろなお お色直し	ねんねん 年々	15　あつ 暑く	さむ 寒く	きこう 気候	あきばれ 秋晴れ
つづ 続きます	じき 時期	こうらく 行楽	かぞくづ 家族連れ	かじゅえん 果樹園	で 出かけ
りんご狩り	のやま 野山	木の実(木の実)		ようちえんじ 幼稚園児	とかい 都会
みせさき 店先	やさい 野菜	くだもの 果物	20　しんまい 新米	ではじ 出始めます	

Wedding Ceremonies and Receptions

A wedding in Japan today is a combination of customs long established since the Muromachi Period (1336—1573). and modern habits influenced by the West. People in the old days placed greater importance on the reception, which continued 3 days and 3 nights, rather than a religious ceremony to announce the marriage and introduce the bride to the community.

The modern reception is performed in a showy way, full of flowers and music. After the introduction of the newlywed couple by the matchmaker, a wedding cake-cutting or "a candle-service" in which the couple go around the guests' tables lighting candles, is celebrated as the high point of the reception. Then the bride retires for *o-iro-naoshi* to change once or twice into a different outfit. Not strictly following the original custom but just as a part of the pageantry, even bridegrooms change today as if at a show.

Forms of Wedding

65%

Shinto Ritual Wedding
神前結婚式

Customarily only a limited number of relatives attend the ceremony in the *Shintō* hall. A priest recites *Shintō* prayers. The couple perform the ceremony of the "Three-times-three Exchange of Nuptial Cups" called "*San-san-ku-do*," and each one offers a spring branch of a sacred tree to a god. All the attendants follow, sipping *sake* together to tighten the kinship of the two families.

25%

Christian Ritual Wedding
キリスト教式結婚式

Even if a couple are not baptized Christians, the number of people who choose a Christian wedding is increasing today. The change in meaning of a wedding, from a family event to a personal one, encourages young people to choose a chapel where anyone may attend to celebrate.

5～6%

Buddist Ritual Wedding
仏前結婚式

A Buddhist monk reads a sutra and gives the couple incensed rosaries, a white one to the bridegroom and a red one to the bride. The couple offer incense to Buddha. The bride drinks *sake* to pledge twice, the groom, once, and the relatives follow to toast.

Average Wedding Expenses　　　　平均結婚総費用

婚約　Engagement　67.3万円　　　挙式　披露宴　　　288.1万円　新婚旅行　Honeymoon　105.8万円
Wedding Ceremoney and Reception

こうけい
合計　　　　¥ 7,562,000
Total

新生活の準備　Preparation for the New Life
295万円

Source: Sanwa Bank 1990

六曜表
Rokuyō
Calendar

One month is divided into 5 *Rokuyō* weeks, each with 6 days. Each day on the lunar calendar is named according to the traditional system, and the corresponding days on the solar calendar are noted.

The *Rokuyō* calendar became popular at the very end of the Edo Period. It is used only in Japan and has no scientific background, yet people tend to stick to it in everyday life even today, such as in choosing a lucky day (*Taian*) to open a new shop or to start to build a new house.

◗先勝……(*Sengachi, Senshō*)
Lucky in the morning. You may do anything, even in haste. Unlucky in the afternoon.

⊖友引……(*Tomobiki*)
Lucky the whole day except at noon. Since *tomobiki* means "to pull friends," no funerals are held this day so the deceased will not pull his friends along into the next world. Public crematories are closed.

◖先負……(*Senmake, Senpu*)
You should not do anything official or in haste. Very lucky in the afternoon.

●仏滅……(*Butsumetsu*)
The most unlucky day. You should not do anything special or important, except attend a funeral.

○大安……(*Taian, Daian*)
The most lucky day. You may do anything. Many weddings are held this day.

◖赤口……(*Jakkō, Jakku*)
The *Jakkō*-god torments people this day. Unlucky the whole day except at noon.

67

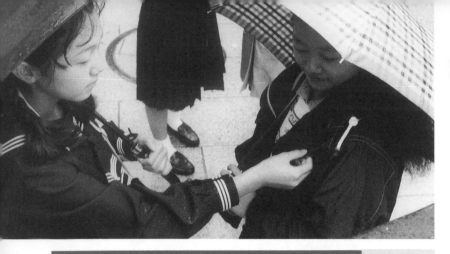

Red Feathers
赤い羽根

In Europe, a red feather has been the symbol of righteousness and courage since the time of Robin Hood. In 1928 Americans in New Orleans began using red feathers for the Community Chest. Japan followed in 1948, offering 10 million red chicken feathers to donors, and 50 million each year today.

"Akai hane" has become one of the autumnal symbols, a recognized seasonal word for *haiku*.

The Red Feather Community Chest Campaign
赤い羽根

In 1921, the first Community Chest Campaign in Japan was carried out. It is a voluntary fund-raising movement of three months duration beginning in October, and it is conducted under a provision of the Social Welfare Service Law enacted in 1951.

Campaigning in public places does not contribute significantly to the total amount raised, but as it creates public awareness and understanding, celebrities volunteer to stand as collectors on October 1st. Every year 2 million people, that is 1 in 60 Japanese, are involved as volunteers.

Field Day
運動会

Field days are usually held on a Sunday so that fathers can attend. It is a family event for those who have elementary schoolchildren. Not only parents but grandparents, brothers and sisters enjoy watching races and games and participating in special programs for the guests. Sunday photographers are busy here and there on the field.

Horse Racing
競 馬

These past several years the JRA (Japan Racing Association) tried to change the image of racing, placing commercial messages in the mass media.

Horse racing such as the Emperor's Cup Horse Race in the spring in Kyoto and in the autumn in Tokyo as well as the Japan Derby are most popular ones. More than 100,000 people enjoy the autumn race, wagering over ¥30 billion, increasing yearly.

Even young women enjoy races today, and the tracks have become popular dating spots.

OCTOBER 10 月

神無月
かんなづき

In October on the lunar calendar, they say, gods all over Japan got together at Izumo in Shimane Prefecture to decide who's going to marry whom. Since no gods stayed in local shrines, people called October "Godless Month" *Kan'nazuki*. But in Izumo, people called the month, *Kamiarizuki*, "Month with the Gods."

October 1st is "change of dress day." This is the day we change from summer to winter uniforms.

The Red Feather Community Chest Campaign also starts on the 1st. Volunteers and students collect donations at public places such as train stations. When a person puts some money into the collection box, the volunteers pin a red feather to the donor's lapel.

October 10th is Health-Sports Day. On October 10th, 1964, the opening ceremony for the Tokyo Olympics was held. In commemoration, this became a day to enjoy sports. Around this day, kindergartens and schools, communities and companies organize field days. Family members pack their *o-bentō* lunches and join in the programs.

Later in the month, there are more sports events such as the Fall Emperor's Cup Horse Race, the Japan Series of professional baseball, and the fall nationwide sports events.

October is a popular month for weddings. A lucky day such as *Taian** is chosen, and weddings are celebrated one after another at hotels, wedding halls, shrines and churches. The style of the wedding ceremony has almost nothing to do with religion. A wedding reception is held right after the ceremony, and nowadays, not only brides but bridegrooms change costumes during the reception, as wedding parties get more elaborate year after year.

In October, it is neither too hot nor too cold; the weather is calm and comfortable. With fine and fresh autumn days one after the other, this is the season for outings. Families venture out to orchards to enjoy pear-picking or apple-picking. On the hills and in the fields, fruits are ripening. Kindergarteners and schoolchildren go out for chestnut-gathering and sweet potato-digging expeditions. At the urban greengrocers', fall fruits and vegetables such as *matsutake* mushrooms, pears, chestnuts and persimmons are displayed in abundance. Newly-harvested rice appears at the store around this time of year. Autumn fishes such as mackerel, sardines and saury pike are also in season.

* An auspicious day (See *Rokuyō* Calendar p.67)

11月
NOVEMBER

霜月（しもつき）

3日　文化の日（ぶんかのひ）
15日　七五三（しちごさん）
23日　勤労感謝の日（きんろうかんしゃのひ）

　11月になるとだんだん寒くなって、日本列島の各地で紅葉が見られます。もみじやいちょうが赤や黄色に色づき始めると、人々は各地の紅葉の名所へ出かけます。もみじ狩りはこの季節の楽しみの一つです。

　3日は「文化の日」で、祝日です。芸術や学術ですぐれた仕事をした人に、皇居で「文化勲章」がおくられます。

　文化の日のころには、展覧会、音楽会、芸術祭が開かれ、学校では学芸会や文化祭が行われます。特に最近は各地に新しくりっぱな美術館やホールができて、いろいろな文化活動がさかんになってきました。

　15日は「七五三」の日です。多くの地方では7オと3オの女の子と、5オの男の子は晴れ着を着て、神社にお参りに行きます。子供たちは「千歳飴（ちとせあめ）」を手に持って、記念写真をとります。そして、家族そろってレストランで食事をしたり家でごちそうを作ったりして、子供の成長を祝います。

　23日は「勤労感謝の日」で、祝日になります。

　またこの月には東京の下町で「酉の市（とりのいち）」が行われます。「くまで」を買って、商売繁盛を願うまつりです。

　酉の市が終わると1年も終わりに近づき、いそがしい年の暮となります。毎年このころには冷たい北風が吹き始め、北海道や東北、北陸地方は本格的な雪の季節を迎えます。関東地方の家庭でも、夏の間かたずけておいたストーブやこたつなど暖房器具を出して、冬のしたくを始めます。

漢字のよみかた

寒く (さむ)	日本列島 (にほんれっとう)	各地 (かくち)	紅葉 (こうよう)	赤 (あか)	黄色 (きいろ)
色づき (いろ)	始める (はじ)	名所 (めいしょ)	出かけます (で)	もみじ狩り (が)	季節 (きせつ)
楽しみ (たの)	一つ (ひと)	3日 (みっか)	文化の日 (ぶんか ひ)	祝日 (しゅくじつ)	芸術 (げいじゅつ)
学術 (がくじゅつ)	5 皇居 (こうきょ)	文化勲章 (ぶんかくんしょう)	展覧会 (てんらんかい)	音楽会 (おんがくかい)	芸術祭 (げいじゅつさい)
開かれ (ひら)	学芸会 (がくげいかい)	文化祭 (ぶんかさい)	行われます (おこな)	特に (とく)	最近 (さいきん)
美術館 (びじゅつかん)	文化活動 (ぶんか かつどう)	七五三 (しちごさん)	地方 (ちほう)	7才 (ななさい)	3才 (さんさい)
5才 (ごさい)	10 晴れ着 (は ぎ)	神社 (じんじゃ)	お参り (まい)	子供たち (こども)	千歳飴 (ちとせあめ)
記念写真 (きねんしゃしん)	家族 (かぞく)	家 (いえ)	作ったり (つく)	成長 (せいちょう)	祝います (いわ)
勤労感謝の日 (きんろうかんしゃ ひ)	祝日 (しゅくじつ)	下町 (したまち)	酉の市 (とり いち)	15 商売繁盛 (しょうばいはんじょう)	願う (ねが)
終わる (お)	近づき (ちか)	年の暮 (とし くれ)	毎年 (まいとし)	冷たい (つめ)	北風 (きたかぜ)
吹き始め (ふ はじ)	北海道 (ほっかいどう)	東北 (とうほく)	北陸地方 (ほくりくちほう)	本格的な (ほんかくてき)	雪 (ゆき)
季節 (きせつ)	迎えます (むか)	関東地方 (かんとうちほう)	家庭 (かてい)	暖房器具 (だんぼうきぐ)	出して (だ)

71

The Order of Culture
文化勲章

Since 1937, the Order of Culture has been presented to those who have made distinguished contributions in the areas of scientific discoveries and inventions, scholastic studies, literature, and the arts such as painting, sculpture, architecture and music. The recipients are selected by the Minister of Education. At the presentation ceremony, held at the Imperial Palace, the recipients and their spouses are requested to wear formal Japanese costume with family crests, or the most formal Western clothes.

Tori no Ichi
酉の市

Tori no Ichi Festivals are held in some shrines in and around the Tokyo area. Originally an autumn harvest festival among farmers who made an offering of *tori* (chicken) to a nearby shrine, it became popular among the townsfolk of Edo during the 17th and 18th Centuries. In return for their offerings, the farmers got a rake from the shrine. People related a rake to the idea of gathering money or wealth, and the festival gradually changed its meaning. Today, it is thought to be a festival for merchants who wish for good business throughout year, and ornamental rakes decorated with many things symbolic of money are sold in the precincts of the shrine on the day of the festival.

Culture Fairs
文化祭

Art festivals and culture festivals play a big part in school life from elementary school up to university. At the festivals, students' art works are displayed; music, dances and dramas are performed; and scientific and scholastic studies are exhibited. Also, food stalls and game shows are very popular.

Shichi-go-san 七五三

On the 15th of November, seven-year-old girls, five-year-old boys and three-year-old girls (and boys in some areas) and their parents go to a shrine to give thanks and pray for the children's happy and healthy growth. The custom originated in the households of the aristocratic and warrior classes, where three-year old girls had a ceremony to mark beginning to grow their hair long; five-year-olds a ceremony of wearing *hakama* (skirt-like pants worn by adult males), and seven-year-olds a ceremony of wearing *kimono* and *obi* (a sash). The custom gradually spread to the townspeople of Edo, the former name of Tokyo, and in the Meiji Period (1868 to 1912), the present custom of *shichi-go-san* became popular.

Chitoseame 千歳飴

Chitoseame, meaning thousand-year candies, are sold at stores to celebrate children's growth and to pray for their longevity. These are red or white stick candies made of sweetened rice flour and maltose and sold in a paper bag with designs symbolizing luck and longevity.

Onsen 温 泉

More than 70 percent of the land in Japan is mountainous, and there are many volcanoes throughout the country. Thus, hot springs are numerous and going to hot spring bath resorts is very popular. Many famous and popular hot spring resorts have modern, high-rise hotels; in other places, people can enjoy the comfort of traditional Japanese inns. Even in remote areas, deep in the mountains, there are one or two small, rustic bath houses to serve hot spring visitors.

73

秋の味、秋の野山
Autumn Food, Flora and Fauna

さんま	Saury
きのこ	Mushroom
松たけ	"Matsutake" mushroom
ぎんなん	Ginkgo nut
かき	Persimmon
くり	Chestnut
なし	Pear
ぶどう	Grapes
新米	Newly harvested rice

コスモス	Cosmos
ききょう	Chinese bellflower
はぎ	Bush clover
すすき	Japanese pampas grass
きんもくせい	Fragrant olive
きく	Chrysanthemum
けいとうそう	Cockscomb
さざんか	Sasanqua
いちょう	Ginkgo
もみじ	Maple

こおろぎ	Cricket
すず虫	"Bell-ring" cricket
松虫	Matsumushi (a kind of cricket)

冬の味、冬の野山
Winter Food, Flora and Fauna

寒ぶり	Yellowtail in season
たら	Cod
ふぐ	Blowfish
かき	Oyster
あらまきさけ	Lightly salted salmon

シクラメン	Cyclamen
ポインセチア	Poinsettia
はぼたん	Ornamental cabbage
ふくじゅそう	Adonis
せんりょう	Senryo (a kind of evergreen bush)
水仙	Narcissus / Daffodil
梅	Japanese plum blossom

りんご	Apple
みかん	Tangerine

よせなべ	Meat, seafood and vegetables cooked in earthen pot
なべもの	Dishes served in the pot
ゆどうふ	Boiled Tōfu served in earthen pot

NOVEMBER　11 月

霜 し も つ き
月

The Japanese almanac says winter begins on the 8th of November, called *Rittō* (Beginning of Winter) and the first snow falls around the 22nd, *Shōsetsu* (Little Snow).

In the Tohoku area, frost starts to form on the ground this month. The name of the month, "Frost Month," *Shimotsuki* gives warning to farmers to prepare for the coming harsh winter.

As November comes, the weather turns gradually colder, and throughout Japan red and yellow leaves appear on trees. When leaves turn red and yellow, people go out to autumn foliage viewing spots. Viewing the autumn leaves is one of the favorite pastimes of the season.

The 3rd is Culture Day, a national holiday. Those who have made outstanding contributions in the arts and scholarship are presented with the Order of Culture in a ceremony at the Imperial Palace.

Around the time of Culture Day, art exhibitions, concerts and art festivals are held, and schools have performing arts and culture fairs. Especially now, many cultural activities have become popular since grand new museums and concert halls have been built in many parts of the country.

The 15th is the day for *Shichi-go-san*. In many areas of the country, seven- and three-year-old girls and five-year-old boys put on formal clothes and make a visit to a shrine. A commemorative photograph is taken of the children holding a bag of special red and white stick candies. Then, families gather to celebrate the children's growth with a special dinner at a restaurant or at home.

The 23rd is Labor Thanksgiving Day, a national holiday.

At the end of the month, The *Tori no Ichi* Festival is held in downtown Tokyo. People wishing for good luck in business buy a decorated "rake" at the festival. With the *Tori no Ichi* Festival over and the end of the year coming soon, the busy season is approaching. Every year about this time the cold north wind begins to blow, and the Hokkaido, Tohoku, and Hokuriku areas are bracing for a full-scale snow season. And even in households in the Kanto area, people are pulling out the heaters and the *kotatsu* they had stored in closets during the summer, and getting ready for winter.

12月 DECEMBER

師走（しわす）

21日ころ　冬至（とうじ）
23日　天皇誕生日（てんのうたんじょうび）
25日　クリスマス
28日　御用納め（ごようおさめ）
31日　大晦日（おおみそか）

　12月は1年のしめくくりの月で、「師走（しわす）」ともいいます。

　上旬にはボーナスが出ます。夏のお中元と同じように、日頃お世話になった人たちに1年間の感謝をこめて「お歳暮」をおくります。お歳暮、クリスマス、お正月などの買い物客でデパートや商店街はにぎわいます。

5　また、「年賀特別郵便取扱」が開始されます。郵便局では元日に年賀状を配達するために、たくさんのアルバイトをやとって準備します。

　22日ころは「冬至（とうじ）」です。この日には、かぼちゃを食べたり、ゆず湯に入ったりします。かぜを予防し、冬を元気にすごせるといわれています。

　学校はこのころから冬休みになります。

10　そして23日は「天皇誕生日」で祝日です。

　25日のクリスマスは祝日ではありませんが、人々は宗教に関係なくクリスマスを楽しみます。町にはクリスマスツリーがかざられ、ジングルベルのメロディーが流れて、おたがいにプレゼントを交換したり、クリスマスケーキを食べたりしてにぎやかにすごします。またこの時期には忘年会もさかんに開かれま

15　す。

　28日は官公庁の御用納めの日です。この日から役所や会社の多くは年末年始の休暇に入ります。

　駅や空港はお正月をふるさとですごす人、海外旅行やスキー場に出かける人でこみあいます。商店街には正月かざりを売る店ができ、食品売り場は正月料

20　理を買う人でいっぱいになります。各家庭では大掃除をして、正月かざりをかざって、新しい年を迎える準備をします。

　31日は「大晦日（おおみそか）」です。人々は夜には年越しそばを食べ、テレビやラジオで中継される全国の有名寺院の「除夜の鐘」を聞きながら、新年を迎えます。

漢字のよみかた

師走 しわす	上旬 じょうじゅん	出ます で	お中元 ちゅうげん	同じ おな	日頃 ひごろ
お世話 せわ	感謝 かんしゃ	お歳暮 せいぼ	買い物客 か ものきゃく	商店街 しょうてんがい	5 年賀 ねんが
特別郵便 とくべつゆうびん	取扱 とりあつかい	開始されます かいし	郵便局 ゆうびんきょく	元日 がんじつ	年賀状 ねんがじょう
配達する はいたつ	準備します じゅんび	冬至 とうじ	ゆず湯 ゆ	入ったり はい	予防し よぼう
10 天皇誕生日 てんのうたんじょうび	祝日 しゅくじつ	宗教 しゅうきょう	関係 かんけい	楽しみます たの	流れて なが
交換したり こうかん	時期 じき	忘年会 ぼうねんかい	開かれ ひら	15 官公庁 かんこうちょう	御用納め ごようおさ
役所 やくしょ	年末年始 ねんまつねんし	休暇 きゅうか	入ります はい	空港 くうこう	海外旅行 かいがいりょこう
スキー場 じょう	出かける で	店 みせ	食品売り場 しょくひん う ば	正月料理 しょうがつりょうり	20 各家庭 かく かてい
大掃除 おおそうじ	迎える むか	準備 じゅんび	大晦日 おおみそか	夜 よる	年越しそば としこ
中継される ちゅうけい	全国 ぜんこく	有名 ゆうめい	寺院 じいん	除夜の鐘 じょや かね	迎えます むか

Shiwasu
師 走

The word *Shiwasu*, made from the *kanji* for "priest" and for "run," derives its meaning from the tradition that in the old days priests visited parishioners at the end of year, so they were busy running from place to place to finish up their duties.

Nowadays, the word "*Shiwasu*" has been replaced by the word "December."

Year-end Sales
歳末大売出し

Special year-end sales are organized everywhere, in shopping quarters, department stores or supermarkets. A lottery sale attracts many shoppers who collect tickets and draw lots. Prizes may be an airline ticket to Hawaii or Hong Kong, a new deluxe car, a fur coat and so on.

Bōnenkai
忘年会

Bōnenkai, literally means a party to help forget the passing year, made from the *kanji* for "forget", "year" and "meeting". Those who are present at the party forget unpleasant memories connected with the passing year, so they can feel relaxed. They spend a few hours drinking or enjoying other entertainment, such as *karaoke*, which has become very popular in recent years. *Karaoke* revelers enjoy singing songs to the accompaniment of video discs. This helps to enliven the party atmosphere.

元日

あけまして
おめでとう
ございます

謹賀新年

本年も
よろしく
お願いします

元日

Nengahagaki
年賀はがき

Exchanging New Year's greeting cards is a very important custom in Japan. People start preparing for this in the middle of November. The Post office sells "New Year's Greeting Cards with Prize" (*otoshidama-tsuki-nengahagaki*).

There are two kinds: cards with three-yen per-card donation and cards with no donation. The donated money goes to different charities. Each card has a lottery number printed on the bottom.

On January 15th of the new year, the winning numbers are drawn and announced on TV, radio and newspapers. People take cards with winning numbers to a nearby post office and exchange them for prizes.

New Year's Greeting Cards with Prize have been issued since 1949.

Mochitsuki
もちつき

Rice cake pounding was a custom at the end of the year. All households used to do *mochitsuki*, but modern Japanese now buy ready-made rice cakes in a package or use electric *mochi*-makers.

Mochi-pounding gatherings to enjoy this old custom are still held in kindergartens. *Mochi* is made from steamed, hot glutinous rice, and is pounded many times in a wooden tub with a wooden pestle.

Okazariuri
おかざり売り

Many kinds of articles connected with New Year's decorations of various sizes, shapes and prices are sold at open-air stalls set up in shrine precincts or at street corners.

All New Year's decorations are hung between the 26th and the 30th. On the 31st, decorations should not be set up. It is called "*ichiya kazari*" (decorations set up overnight) and is not favored.

Ōmisoka
大晦日

At the end of the year, people begin preparations to welcome the New Year. Housecleaning is as important as the preparation of New Year's food and decorations.

In the old days when people used charcoal fires or firewood to heat their homes, they dumped all the soot (*susu*) at the end of the year. This tradition remains today as the year-end big cleaning.

In households, people clean the whole house by sweeping out dust and doing small repairs, including replacing the old, ripped paper of *shōji* screens with new sheets of paper.

After cleaning the house, people are considered fit, physically and spiritually, to welcome the god of the incoming year.

Toshikoshi Soba
年越しそば

Soba (buckwheat noodles) symbolize long life because of their long shape, so *soba* is eaten on New Year's Eve with the hope for a life as long as a noodle in the coming years.

New Year's Eve is the busiest day at *soba* restaurants and *soba* shops. The custom of eating *toshikoshi soba* started during the Edo Period.

Joya no Kane   除夜の鐘

The custom of ringing out the old year with temple bells on New Year's Eve has been observed since the Nara Period. Traditionally, priests took turns striking the temple bells 108 times in succession, but nowadays many temples afford an opportunity to anybody who wants to strike the bell, which has the power to drive away evil. According to Buddhist belief, the 108 peals of the temple bell represent the 108 evil passions that beset mankind. When the last peal sounds, these earthly desires of human beings are cast out. Thus, people greet the New Year in a pure state of mind.

DECEMBER 　12 月

師し
走わ
　す

The characters that form this word, *Shiwasu*, mean, "Priests are running." That shows how busy people are at the end of the year.

December is the month for final settlements, and is also called *Shiwasu*.

Bonuses are given out at the beginning of December. The same as *o-chūgen* in summer, people send *o-seibo* gifts to express grateful feelings to people who have been kind to them throughout the year. *O-seibo*, Christmas and New Year's shoppers throng department stores and shopping streets.

On the 15th, the post office begins accepting New Year's cards for delivery on New Year's Day. Post offices employ extra staff to be able to deliver all the cards on the 1st of January.

Around the 22nd is the Winter Solstice. On this day people eat pumpkin and take a hot bath with a *yuzu* orange steeped in it. It is said to prevent colds and get one through the winter in good health.

Schools let out around this day for winter vacation.

The 23rd is the birthday of the Emperor, and is a national holiday.

Christmas on the 25th is not a national holiday, but people enjoy Christmas no matter what their religion. Towns are decorated with Christmas trees, the melody of Jingle Bells floats on the air, and people spend the day merrily giving each other presents and eating Christmas cakes.

Year-end parties are held at this time.

The 28th is the last work day of the year for government and municipal offices. On this day most of the public offices and private companies begin vacations that last through the New Year.

At train stations and airports, people who will spend the New Year in their hometowns are crowded together with those setting out to foreign countries or to ski areas. On shopping streets, shops for New Year's decorations are set up, and food counters are packed with people buying New Year's special items. In every household, people are cleaning house, making New Year's decorations and preparing to greet the New Year.

The 31st is New Year's Eve. That night people eat *toshikoshi soba*, listen for *Joya no Kane** broadcast at midnight on TV and radio from famous temples all over the country, and welcome the New Year.

* New Year's Eve Bells

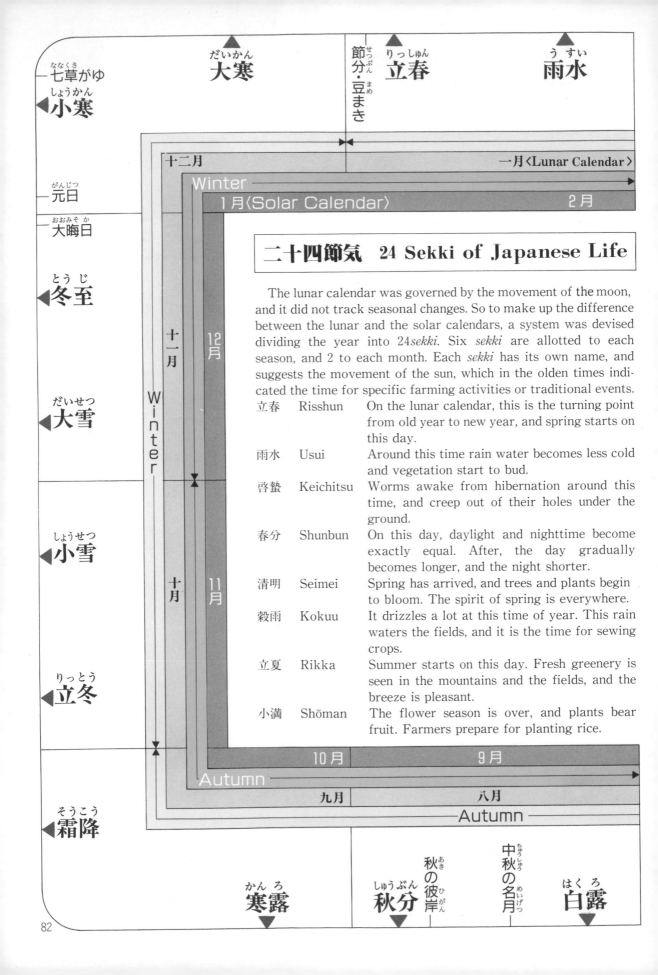

七草がゆ（ななくさがゆ）
小寒（しょうかん）◀
大寒（だいかん）▲
節分・豆まき（せつぶん・まめまき）▲
立春（りっしゅん）▲
雨水（うすい）▲

元日（がんじつ）
大晦日（おおみそか）
冬至（とうじ）◀
大雪（だいせつ）◀
小雪（しょうせつ）◀
立冬（りっとう）◀
霜降（そうこう）◀

十二月
一月〈Lunar Calendar〉
Winter
1月〈Solar Calendar〉
2月

十一月
十月
12月
11月
Winter

10月
9月
Autumn
九月
八月
Autumn

寒露（かんろ）▼
秋分（しゅうぶん）▼
秋の彼岸（あきのひがん）
中秋の名月（ちゅうしゅうのめいげつ）
白露（はくろ）▼

二十四節気　24 Sekki of Japanese Life

The lunar calendar was governed by the movement of the moon, and it did not track seasonal changes. So to make up the difference between the lunar and the solar calendars, a system was devised dividing the year into 24 *sekki*. Six *sekki* are allotted to each season, and 2 to each month. Each *sekki* has its own name, and suggests the movement of the sun, which in the olden times indicated the time for specific farming activities or traditional events.

立春	Risshun	On the lunar calendar, this is the turning point from old year to new year, and spring starts on this day.
雨水	Usui	Around this time rain water becomes less cold and vegetation start to bud.
啓蟄	Keichitsu	Worms awake from hibernation around this time, and creep out of their holes under the ground.
春分	Shunbun	On this day, daylight and nighttime become exactly equal. After, the day gradually becomes longer, and the night shorter.
清明	Seimei	Spring has arrived, and trees and plants begin to bloom. The spirit of spring is everywhere.
穀雨	Kokuu	It drizzles a lot at this time of year. This rain waters the fields, and it is the time for sewing crops.
立夏	Rikka	Summer starts on this day. Fresh greenery is seen in the mountains and the fields, and the breeze is pleasant.
小満	Shōman	The flower season is over, and plants bear fruit. Farmers prepare for planting rice.

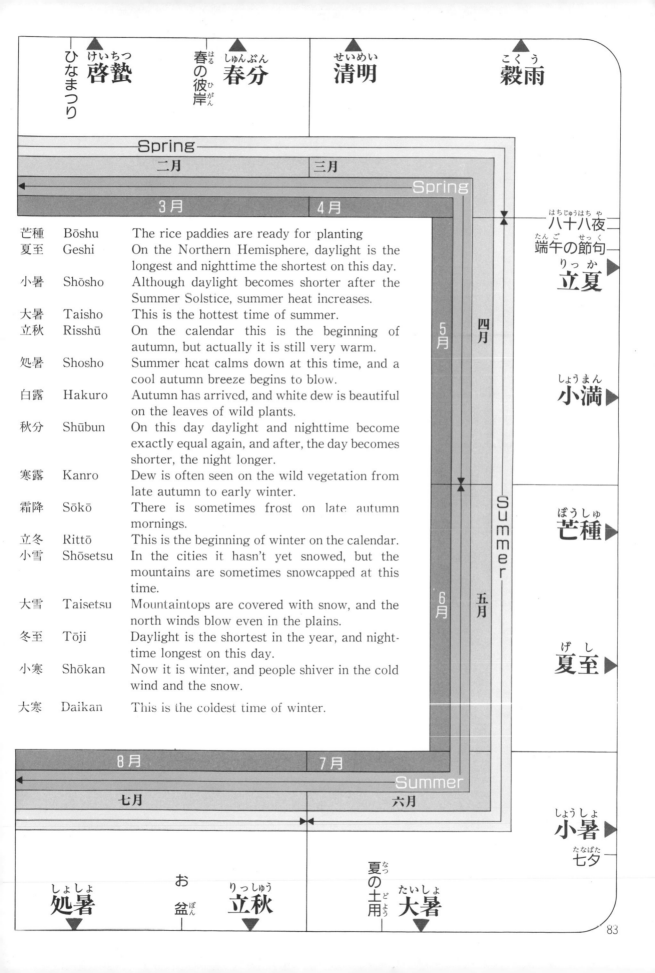

　本文中の語で、初級終了段階の学習者には難しいと思われる語は、すべて本文中にあらわれる順に語彙リストに収録し、英訳をつけた。学習者の便宜を図り、既出の語も各月ごとにそのつど提出してある。

　見出し語は本文中の形のままとし、動詞の場合はその辞書形を合わせて載せた。ただし、動詞て形で副詞的に使われているもの（*sorotte, matomete*）やた形で形容詞的に使われているもの（*hanayaida, sugureta*）は辞書形を併記しない。い―形容詞とな―形容詞は本文中の形のみ載せてある。

　語彙表のローマ字表記に関しては、以下の原則によった。

Ⅰ．動詞
　　1．動詞のます形はひとつづりとする。
　　　　iwaimasu, kazarimasu
　　2．て形にいる、くるなどが付いたものは、て形の後にスペースを入れる。
　　　　tsutaerarete imasu, chikazuite kimasu
　　3．漢語＋するはするの前にスペースを入れる。
　　　　shusseki shimasu, haitatsu shimasu
　　4．複合動詞は間にスペースを入れる。
　　　　saki hajimemasu, ukabi agarimasu

Ⅱ．名詞
　　1．祝祭日や特別な行事の名前は語頭を大文字とする。
　　　　Kenpō Kinenbi, Bōsai no Hi
　　2．接頭語、接尾語はハイフンでつなぐ。
　　　　o-toso, Hyōgo-ken, shi-gatsu
　　　　ただし、ひとつづりにした方がわかりやすい語や、すでに接頭語をともなって慣用が固定している語にはハイフンを入れない。
　　　　jukensei, mayonaka, otoshidama
　　3．複合語（四字熟語など）は語構成に合わせて分かち書きをする。
　　　　nenmatsu nenshi, natsuyama tozan, arabia sūji
　　　　ただし、ひとつづりにした方が分かりやすいものには、スペースを入れない。
　　　　sofubo, bokinbako, ongakukai

Ⅲ．長音
　　長音は母音字の上に長音符号「‐」をつけて、あらわす。
　　　　kenshū, ryōshin
　　ただし、い列長音は*ii*、え列長音は*ei*とする。
　　　　sukiijō, seijinshiki
　　外来語のえ列長音は*ē*によってあらわす。
　　　　mēdē

Ⅳはつ音
　　はつ音（*n*）が母音字（*a, i, u, e, o*）、*y*および*n*の直前に来る時は、*n*がはつ音であることを示し、読みやすくするためにアポストロフィーをつける。
　　　　toshion'na, shin'nen, Nihon'ichi

Vocabulary List

All words that may be difficult for pre-intermediate-level students are listed in the vocabulary list as they appear in the main text of each month's story. The corresponding dictionary forms are also listed for verbs. However, the dictionary forms are not listed for the Te-form of a verb which is used as an adverb (e.g. *sorotte*, *matomete*) or for the Ta-form of a verb which is used as an adjective (e.g. *hanayaida*, *sugureta*). I—adjectives and Na—adjectives are given in the forms which appear in the text.

The Romanization of the words follows the following rules.

I. Verbs
1. A verb in its *masu*-form is written as one word.
   iwaimasu, kazarimasu
2. Te-form of a verb plus *iru, kuru*, etc., is written with a space between V—te and *iru, kuru*, etc.
   tsutaerarete imasu, chikazuite kimasu
3. A verb consisting of a Chinese compound and *suru* is written with a space between the Chinese compound and *suru*.
   shusseki shimasu, haitatsu shimasu
4. A compound verb is written with a space between the first element and the second element.
   saki hajimemasu, ukabi agarimasu

II. Nouns
1. The words designating national holidays, special memorial days and other special event days are listed with a capital letter at the beginning of the word.
   Kempō Kinenbi, Bōsai no Hi
2. A word with a prefix or a suffix is written with a hyphen between the prefix or the suffix and the word.
   o-toso, Hyogo-ken, shi-gatsu
   However, a hyphen is omitted if its absence facilitates understanding of the word as in the case of *jukensei* and *mayonaka*. Also, for words that are always used with the honorifics *o* or *go* are written without a hyphen, for example, *otoshidama*.
3. Compound words such as words made from four Chinese characters are written with a space between each word.
   nenmatsu nenshi, natsuyama tozan, arabia sūji
   However, compounds which are easier to understand if they are written as one word are written accordingly.
   sofubo, bokinbako, ongakukai

III. Long Vowels
   Long vowels are indicated by putting a line over the vowel, except for long *i* which is written as *ii*, and *e* which is written as *ei*.
   kenshū, ryōshin, but *sukiijō, seijinshiki*
   For loanwords, a long *e* is indicated by a line over the *e*.
   mēdē

IV. Syllabic *n*
   When a syllabic *n* appears just before *a, i u, e, o, y* or *n*, an apostrophe is put after the syllabic *n* to facilitate the reading of the word.
   toshion'na, shin'nen, Nihon'ichi

1月

P. ℓ.

8 1 元日	ganjitsu	the first day of the year, New Year's Day	
表す	arawasu	to signify	
正月	shōgatsu	The New Year holiday period	
玄関	genkan	entranceway	
門	mon	gate	
正月かざり	shōgatsu kazari	New Year's decorations	
昔	mukashi	ancient times, long time ago	
門松	kadomatsu	a kind of New Year's decoration	(→P. 10)
しめかざり	shimekazari	a kind of New Year's decoration	(→P. 10)
ドアー用の輪かざり	doayō no wakazari	wreath on the door	
5 元旦	gantan	morning of New Year's Day	
家族	kazoku	family	
そろって	sorotte	together	
お－とそ	o-toso	spiced *sake* with medical herbs	(→P. 10)
お－ぞうに	o-zōni	New Year's special dish	(→P. 10)
おせち料理	osechi ryōri	New Year's special dishes	(→P. 10)
新年	shin'nen	New Year	
祝います	iwaimasu	祝う to celebrate	
両親	ryōshin	parents	
お年玉	otoshidama	New Year's monetary gift to children from parents and visitors	(→P. 11)
人々	hitobito	people	
幸せ	shiawase	happiness	
願って	negatte	願う to wish	
神社	jinja	shrine	
寺院	jiin	temple	
初詣	hatsumōde	the year's first visit to a temple or a shrine	(→P. 11)
伝統的な	dentōteki na	traditional	
行事	gyōji	event	
最近	saikin	nowadays	
ホテル	hoteru	hotel	
温泉地	onsenchi	spa resort	
スキー場	sukiijō	ski resort	
海外	kaigai	overseas	
すごす	sugosu	to spend	
10 年賀状	nengajō	New Year's greeting card	(→P. 79)

10 まとめて	matomete	all at once	
配達されます	haitatsu saremasu	配達する to deliver	
あいさつ	aisatsu	greeting	
年	toshi	year	
えと	eto	each year in a cycle of 12 years that bears the name of a zodiac animal	(→P. 17)
写真	shashin	photograph	
印刷した	insatsu shita	印刷する to print	
楽しみ	tanoshimi	pleasure	
正月三が日	shōgatsu sanganichi	the first three days of the New Year	
役所	yakusho	government and municipal offices	
商店	shōten	store	
親類	shinrui	relative	
知人	chijin	acquaintance	
上司	jōshi	superior at the office or company	
年始回り	nenshimawari	to go around on New Year's visits	
15 官公庁	kankōchō	government and municipal offices (approximately same as *yakusho*)	
御用始め	goyōhajime	the first day of work for government and municipal offices	
年末年始	nenmatsu nenshi	年末 year-end 年始 New Year 年末年始 year-end and New Year	
休暇	kyūka	holiday	
仕事始め	shigotohajime	date to begin work	
七草がゆ	nanakusagayu	rice porridge with seven spring herbs	
習慣	shūkan	custom	
古くから	furuku kara	since olden times	
春の七草	haru no nanakusa	seven spring herbs	(→P.11)
お－かゆ	o-kayu	rice porridge, rice gruel	
健康	kenkō	health	
伝えられています	tsutaerarete imasu	伝える to pass on	
20 成人の日	Seijin no Hi	Coming-of-Age Day	
二十歳	hatachi	20 years old	
成人式	Seijinshiki	Coming-of-Age Ceremony	(→P. 12)
行います	okonaimasu	行う to hold	
中旬	chūjun	the middle ten days of the month, midmonth	
大相撲初場所	ōzumō hatsubasho	the year's first *sumō* wrestling tournament	(→P. 12)

両国国技館	Ryōgoku Kokugikan	National Sports Indoor Arena at Ryogoku in Tokyo
熱戦	nessen	tough competition
優勝者	yūshōsha	winner
決まります	kimarimasu	決まる to be decided
大寒	daikan	the coldest day of the year according to the lunar calendar (→P. 82)
松の内	matsu no uchi	during the first seven days of the New Year
はなやいだ	hanayaida	merry
気分	kibun	mood
さらに	sarani	further
きびしく	kibishiku	bitter

2月

P. ℓ. 14 1	北海道	Hokkaidō	Hokkaido
	日本海側	Nihonkaigawa	the Japan Sea costal areas
	各地	kakuchi	many places, all parts
	雪まつり	yukimatsuri	snow festival (→P. 16)
	行われます	okonawaremasu	行う to hold
	札幌	Sapporo	Sapporo
	数メートル	sū-mētoru	many meters
	像	zō	statue
	建物	tatemono	building
	もけい	mokei	replica
	観光客	kankōkyaku	tourists
	日本各地	Nihon kakuchi	all parts of Japan
	外国	gaikoku	foreign countries
	おとずれます	otozuremasu	おとずれる to visit
5	西高東低	seikō tōtei	high (pressure) in the west, low (pressure) in the east
	気圧配置	kiatsu haichi	気圧 atmospheric pressure, 配置 pattern 気圧配置 atmospheric pressure pattern (→P. 16)
	ゆるむ	yurumu	to weaken, to get loose
	中旬	chūjun	the middle ten days of the month, midmonth
	なれない	narenai	なれる to be accustomed
	つもる	tsumoru	to pile on

交通	kōtsū	traffic	
混乱したり	konran shitari	混乱する to be disrupted, to be in a mess	
こおった	kootta	こおる to be frozen	
すべって	subette	すべる to slip	
けが人	keganin	the wounded	
若者	wakamono	young people	
人気がある	ninki ga aru	to be popular	
スポーツ	supōtsu	sport	
スキー場	sukiijō	ski area	
にぎわい	nigiwai	にぎわう to be crowded	
リフト	rifuto	chairlift	
行列	gyōretsu	line	
10 受験シーズン	juken shiizun	受験 taking an entrance examination	
		シーズン (season in English) time	
		受験シーズン time for taking entrance	
		examinations	
大学	daigaku	university, college	
高校	kōkō	high school	
私立	shiritsu	private	
国立	kokuritsu	national	
中学	chūgaku	junior high school	
入学試験	nyūgaku shiken	入学 entrance into school. 試験 examination	
		入学試験 entrance examination	
競争	kyōsō	competition	
きびしい	kibishii	hard, difficult	
受験地獄	juken jigoku	examination hell	
節分	setsubun	the turning point from winter to spring	
		on the lunar calendar	
こよみ	koyomi	calendar	(→P. 82)
季節	kisetsu	season	
わかれる	wakareru	to turn to	
鬼	oni	evil spirits	
追い払って	oiharatte	追い払う to drive away	
迎える	mukaeru	to celebrate	
豆まき	mamemaki	bean-throwing rite	(→P. 17)
神社	jinja	shrine	
お寺	o-tera	temple	
15 年男	toshiotoko	man born under the same zodiac sign as the current year	(→P. 17)

15	年女	toshion'na	woman born under the same zodiac sign as the current year (→P. 17)
	各家庭	kaku katei	each home
	鬼は外，福は内	oni wa soto, fuku wa uchi	"Evil spirits outside, good luck within"
	年令	nenrei	age
	同じ	onaji	same
	数	kazu	number
	健康	kenkō	health
	信じられています	shinjirarete imasu	信じる to believe
	立春	risshun	the first day of spring
	意味します	imi shimasu	意味する to mean
	気温	kion	temperature
	梅	ume	plum blossom
	水仙	suisen	daffodil
	咲き始め	saki hajime	咲き始める to begin to bud
	冷たい	tsumetai	chilly
	空気	kūki	air
	香り	kaori	fragrance
	ただよいます	tadayoimasu	ただよう to float
20	以後	igo	after
	春一番	haruichiban	the first southern storm of the year
	ふきあれます	fukiaremasu	ふきあれる to rage
	つげる	tsugeru	to tell
	強い	tsuyoi	strong
	南風	minamikaze	the south wind
	一歩一歩	ip-po ip-po	step by step, gradually
	人々	hitobito	people
	心待ちにします	kokoromachi ni shimasu	心待ちにする to long for
	一輪	ichi-rin	one twig
	嵐雪	Ransetsu	服部嵐雪 Hattori Ransetsu (1654－1707) *haiku* poet in the Edo Period (→P. 18)

3月

P. ℓ.			
20 1	弥生	Yayoi	another old name for March
	ますます	masumasu	more and more
	成長する	seichō suru	to grow

意味	imi	meaning	
ひなまつり	Hinamatsuri	Hina Doll Festival	(→P. 22)
ひな人形	hinaningyō	special dolls for Hina Doll Festival	(→P. 22)
かざり	kazari	かざる to display	
ももの花	momo no hana	peach blossoms	
なの花	nanohana	rape blossoms	
生けます	ikemasu	生ける to arrange (floweres)	
ちらし寿司	chirashizushi	vinegared rice mixed with various vegetables and fishes	(→P. 22)
はまぐり	hamaguri	clam	
吸い物	suimono	clear soup	
ひなあられ	hina arare	popped, sugar coated rice and rice cake cubes for Hina Doll Festival	
白酒	shirozake	almost non-alcoholic white sweet *sake* for children	
5 用意して	yōi shite	用意する to prepare	
親戚	shinseki	relative	
まねいて	maneite	まねく to invite	
耳の日	Mimi no Hi	Ears Day	(→P. 23)
アラビア数字	arabia sūji	Arabic numerals	
形	katachi	shape	
似ている	nite iru	似る to resemble	
健康	kenkō	health	
卒業式	sotsugyōshiki	commencement	(→P. 24)
終業式	shūgyōshiki	school term closing ceremony	
行われます	okonawaremasu	行う to hold	
幼稚園	yōchien	kindergarten	
大学	daigaku	university	
最終学年	saishū gakunen	最終 the last, 学年 grade 最終学年 the last grade, graduating grade	
生徒	seito	student	
卒業証書	sotsugyō shōsho	卒業 graduation, 証書 certificate 卒業証書 certificate, diploma	
10 お-世話になった	o-sewa ni natta	世話になる to be taken care of, to be shown kindness	
感謝	kansha	appreciation	
気持	kimochi	feeling	
表して	arawashite	表す to show	

10	謝恩会	shaonkai	graduation party, a party given by graduates in honor of their teachers
	開かれます	hirakaremasu	開く to give, to hold
	父母	fubo	father and mother, parents
	参加する	sanka suru	to participate
	春休み	haruyasumi	spring holidays, spring recess
	決算期	kessanki	fiscal term
			In Japan one fiscal year is from April to March the next year.
	あたる	ataru	to fall on
	所得税確定申告	shotokuzei kakutei shinkoku	income tax fiscal declaration
	区切り	kugiri	the end
	転勤	tenkin	job transfer within the same company but to different location (→P. 24)
	転校	tenkō	transfer to another school
15	引越	hikkoshi	moving to new house
	季節	kisetsu	season
	真夜中	mayonaka	midnight
	奈良	Nara	Nara City
	東大寺	Tōdaiji	a Kegon sect temple in Nara City, built in the 8th Century by Emperor Shomu's order
	二月堂	Nigatsudō	one of the temple buldings at Todaiji Temple
	お水取り	Omizutori	Water-drawing Ceremony, a part of the monks' training program at Todaiji Temple (→P. 23)
	行われます	okonawaremasu	行う to hold
	関西地方	Kansai chihō	Kansai area
	つげる	tsugeru	to tell
	行事	gyōji	event
	春分の日	Shunbun no Hi	the Spring Equinox
	前後	zengo	around
	お-彼岸	o-higan	a week around the Equinox
	家族	kazoku	family
	そろって	sorotte	together
	お-墓参り	o-hakamairi	visiting the graves of one's ancestors (→P. 24)
20	昔	mukashi	in the old days, ancient times

4月

(→P. 28)
(→P. 30)
(→P. 29)

P. ℓ.

26 1 気温	kion	temperature
北海道	Hokkaidō	Hokkaido
東北地方	Tōhoku chihō	Tohoku area
関東地方	Kantō chihō	Kanto area
以南	inan	to the south of
桜	sakura	cherry trees / blossoms
やまぶき	yamabuki	a rose-like shrub that has yellow flowers in spring
咲き始めます	saki hajimemasu	咲き始める to begin to bud
始業式	shigyōshiki	school term opening ceremony
新学期	shingakki	new term
5 新入生	shin'nyūsei	freshman, new student
入学式	nyūgakushiki	school entrance ceremony
行います	okonaimasu	行う to hold
校長先生	kōchōsensei	school principal
それぞれ	sorezore	each
紹介	shōkai	introduction
両親	ryōshin	parents
祖父母	sofubo	grandparents
ランドセル	randoseru	backpack-type book bag
入社式	nyūshashiki	company's entrance ceremony for new recruits
スーツ	sūtsu	business suit
新入社員	shin'nyū shain	new recruit
激励	gekirei	encouragement
前後	zengo	around the time of
10 研修	kenshū	training (sessions)
プロ野球	puro yakyū	professional baseball
開幕	kaimaku	opening
開幕戦	kaimakusen	opening game
ファン	fuan	fan
お-花見	o-hanami	flower viewing
季節	kisetsu	season
楽しむ	tanoshimu	to enjoy
伝統的な	dentōteki na	traditional
行事	gyōji	event

	沖縄	Okinawa	Okinawa
	九州	Kyūshū	Kyushu
	四国	Shikoku	Shikoku
	本州	Honshū	Honshu, the Main Island of Japan
	咲き出し	saki dashi	咲き出す to come into bloom
15	開花時期	kaika jiki	開花 blooming, 時期 time, 開花時期 time of blooming
	示す	shimesu	to show, to indicate
	桜前線	sakura zensen	cherry blossom front (→P. 29)
	動き	ugoki	progress, movement
	ようす	yōsu	manner
	天気予報	tenki yohō	weather report
	人々	hitobito	people
	お-弁当	o-bentō	lunch box
	名所	meisho	spot, famous for
	おとずれ	otozure	おとずれる to visit
	夜空	yozora	night sky
	浮び上がる	ukabi agaru	to be outlined, to be lit up
	夜桜	yozakura	cherry blossoms in the evening
	風情	fuzei	taste
	にぎやかに	nigiyaka ni	merrily
	すごす	sugosu	to pass time
20	若葉	wakaba	young leaves
	みどりの日	Midori no Hi	Greenery Day
	祝日	shukujitsu	national holiday
	4月の末	shi-gatsu no sue	the end of April
	振替休日	furikae kyūjitsu	designated holiday
	加わる	kuwawaru	to be added
	大型連休	ōgata renkyū	big scale holiday week

5月

P. ℓ.

32	1 さわやかで	sawayaka de	splendid, refreshing
	新緑	shinryoku	fresh, green foliage
	季節	kisetsu	season
	晴天	seiten	sunny weather
	五月晴れ	satsukibare	sunny days of May

遠足	ensoku	excursion	
運動会	undōkai	athletic meeting	(→P. 68)
メーデー	Mēdē	May Day	
祭典	saiten	festival	
各地	kakuchi	all parts, many places	
催し物	moyooshimono	event	
5 憲法記念日	Kenpō Kinenbi	憲法 Constitution, 記念日 Memorial Day 憲法記念日 Constitution Day	
国民の休日	kokumin no kyūjitsu	nationwide vacation day	
子供の日	Kodomo no Hi	Children's Day	
三連休	san-renkyu	three consecutive holidays	
みどりの日	Midori no Hi	Greenery Day	
ゴールデンウイーク	Gōruden Uiiku	Golden Week	
家族	kazoku	family	
旅行したり	ryoko shitari	旅行する to travel	
潮干狩り	shiohigari	clam gathering at low tide	(→P. 35)
スポーツ	supōtsu	sports	
戸外	kogai	outdoor	
楽しみます	tanoshimimasu	楽しむ to enjoy	
出かける	dekakeru	to go out	
行楽地	korakuchi	resorts	
道路	dōro	road	
大混雑	dai-konzatsu	to be packed	
10 正月	shōgatsu	New Year's holiday period	
夏休み	natsuyasumi	summer vacation	
海外旅行	kaigai ryokō	海外 overseas, 旅行 travel (→P. 36) 海外旅行 overseas travel	
海外旅行者	kaigai ryokōsha	海外 overseas, 旅行者 traveller 海外旅行者 people traveling overseas (→P. 37)	
年間	nenkan	annually	
1990年現在	sen kyūhyaku kyūjū-nen genzai	the latest data of 1990 現在 at present	
こえています	koete imasu	こえる to exceed	
昔	mukashi	ancient times	
端午の節句	Tango no Sekku	Boy's Festival, Boy's Day	
成長	seichō	growth	
現在	genzai	nowadays, at present	
祝う	iwau	to celebrate	

15 こいのぼり	koinobori	carp streamer	(→P. 34)
五月人形	gogatsuningyō	*samurai* or warrior doll	(→P. 34)
かぶと	kabuto	warrior's helmet	(→P. 34)
かざります	kazarimasu	かざる to display	
しょうぶ湯	shōbuyu	bath with iris leaves	(→P. 34)
ちまき	chimaki	dumpling of sweet rice wrapped in bamboo leaves	
かしわもち	kashiwamochi	rice powder cake with sweet bean paste filling wrapped in an oak leaf	
風習	fūshū	custom	
母の日	Haha no Hi	Mother's Day	
カーネーション	kānēshon	carnation	
プレゼント	purezento	present, gift	
おくり	okuri	おくる to give	
感謝	kansha	gratitude	
気持ち	kimochi	feeling	
表します	arawashimasu	表す to express	
新茶	shincha	newly harvested tea	(→P. 35)
八十八夜	hachijūhachiya	the eighty-eighth day after the beginning of spring (*Risshun*)	
新芽	shinme	new, young leaves	
香り	kaori	fragrance	
20 うまみ	umami	flavor	
喜ばれます	yorokobaremasu	喜ぶ to prize	

6月

P. ℓ. 38 1 しょうぶ	shōbu	iris	
あじさい	ajisai	hydrangea	
雨に洗われた	ame ni arawareta	雨に洗われる to glisten in the rain	
青葉	aoba	green leaves	
季節	kisetsu	season	
気温	kion	temperature	
蒸し暑い	mushiatsui	humid	
気候	kikō	climate	
衣替え	koromogae	change of dress	(→P. 40)
制服	seifuku	uniform	

いっせいに	isseini	all at once, all together	
夏服	natsufuku	summer uniform, summer clothes	
とりかえます	torikaemasu	とりかえる to change	
下旬	gejun	the last ten days of the month	
		the latter part of the month	
5 つゆ	tsuyu	rainy season	
梅の実	ume no mi	plum	
熟す	jukusu	to ripen	
オホーツク海高気圧	Ohōtsukukai kōkiatsu	high pressure system over the Okhotsk Sea	
太平洋高気圧	Taiheiyō kōkiatsu	high pressure system over the Pacific Ocean	
衝突して	shōtotsu shite	衝突する to collide	
梅雨前線	baiu zensen	梅雨 rainy season, 前線 front, (→P 40)	
		梅雨前線 seasonal rain front	
気象庁	Kishōchō	the Meteorological Agency	
梅雨入り宣言	tsuyuiri sengen	梅雨入り beginning of rainy season,	
		宣言 announcement,	
		梅雨入り宣言 announcement of the official	
		beginning of rainy season	
時期	jiki	time	
地方	chihō	location, area	
10 北海道	Hokkaidō	Hokkaido	
不快	fukai	unpleasant	
農業用水	nōgyō yōsui	農業 agriculture, 用水 water for	
		農業用水 water for agriculture	
生活用水	seikatsu yōsui	生活 living, life 用水 water for	
		生活用水 water for daily life	
めぐみ	megumi	blessing	
稲作農家	inasaku nōka	稲作 rice growing, 農家 farmer	
		稲作農家 rice growing farmer	
田植え	taue	rice planting (→P. 42)	
梅酒	umeshu	plum brandy	
梅干し	umeboshi	pickled plums	
つけたり	tsuketari	つける to pickle	
１年中で	ichinenjū de	in a year	
昼間	hiruma	daytime	
夏至	Geshi	Summer Solstice	
15 冬至	Tōji	Winter Solstice	
役所	yakusho	goverment and municipal offices	

ボーナス	bōnasu	bonus	(→P. 41)
給料	kyūryō	salary	
給与振込	kyūyo furikomi	給与 salary,　振込 transfer, 給与振込 bank account transfer of salary	

7月

各地	kakuchi	various places	
海開き	umibiraki	opening of the ocean beach to swimmers	
山開き	yamabiraki	opening of the mountain to climbers	
行われ	okonaware	行う to hold	
海水浴	kaisuiyoku	sea bathing	
夏山登山	natsuyama tozan	mountaineering in summer	
シーズン	shiizun	season	
七夕	Tanabata	Star Festival	(→P. 46)
伝説	densetsu	legend	
はたおり姫	hataorihime	weaver	
織女星	Shokujosei	Vega	
恋人	koibito	sweetheart	
牛飼い	ushikai	cowherd	
牽牛星	Kengyūsei	Altair	
たった	tatta	only	
天の川	Amanogawa	the Milky Way	(→P. 46)
5　たんざく	tanzaku	narrow paper strip for writing a poem	
願いごと	negaigoto	wish	
ささ竹	sasatake	small bamboo tree	
つるします	tsurushimasu	つるす to hang	
おり紙	origami	square colored paper for folding	
くさり	kusari	chain made with connected paper strips	
かざります	kazarimasu	かざる to decorate	
中旬	chūjun	the middle ten days of the month,　midmonth	
梅雨前線	baiu zensen	seasonal rain front	(→P. 40)
北上する	hokujō suru	to go (up) north	
消える	kieru	to disappear	
気象庁	Kishōchō	the Meteorological Agency	
梅雨明け宣言	tsuyuake sengen	梅雨明け the end of the rainy season, 宣言 announcement,　梅雨明け宣言 official announcement for the end of the rainy season	

明ける	akeru	to be over	
いよいよ	iyoiyo	finally	
本格的な	honkakuteki na	real	
最高気温	saikō kion	最高 the highest, 気温 temperature	
		最高気温 the highest temperature	
30度	sanjū-do	30 degrees	
こえる	koeru	to exceed	
真夏日	manatsubi	high summer day	
明け方	akegata	dawn	
最低気温	saitei kion	最低 the lowest, 気温 temperature	
		最低気温 the lowest temperature	
以下	ika	below	
熱帯夜	nettaiya	tropical night	
続きます	tsuzukimasu	続く to continue	
10 土用	doyō	the hottest period of summer	
丑の日	Ushi no Hi	Day of the Cow	(→P. 47)
夏バテ	natsubate	energy-draining effect of the summer heat	
うなぎのかば焼き	unagi no kabayaki	broiled eel	(→P. 47)
風習	fūshū	custom	
需要	juyō	demand	
ふえる	fueru	to increase	
日頃	higoro	usually	
お-世話になった	o-sewa ni natta	世話になる to be taken care of	
		to be shown kindness	
人々	hitobito	people	
おくり物	okurimono	gift	
習慣	shūkan	custom	
お-中元	o-chūgen	midsummer gift	(→P. 47)
デパート	depāto	department store	
商店街	shōtengai	shopping area	
中元大売り出し	chūgen ō-uridashi	special midsummer gift sale	
にぎわいます	nigiwaimasu	にぎわう to be crowded	
15 上旬	jōjun	the first ten days of the month	
		the first part of the month	
暑中見舞い	shochū mimai	midsummer greeting	(→P. 47)
はがき	hagaki	post card	
暮している	kurashite iru	暮す to spend	
たずねます	tazunemasu	たずねる to inquire after	

Ｉ学期	ichi-gakki	the first school term
終業式	shūgyōshiki	term closing ceremony
小学校	shōgakkō	elementary school
通知表	tsūchihyō	report card
約	yaku	about
夏休み	natsuyasumi	summer vacation
宿題	shukudai	homework, assignment
家族	kazoku	family
20 野外活動	yagai katsudō	野外 outdoor, 活動 activity, 野外活動 outdoor activity
合宿	gasshuku	training camp
旅行	ryokō	travel
出かけます	dekakemasu	出かける to go out
大学	daigaku	university
高校	kōkō	high school
受験生	jukensei	examinee
集中して	shūchū shite	intensively
受験勉強	juken benkyō	studying in preparation for the entrance examination
予備校	yobikō	cram school
塾	juku	private tutoring school
夏期講習	kaki kōshū	summer course for preparation for the entrance examination (→P. 48)
出席します	shusseki shimasu	出席する to attend

8月

P. ℓ. 50 Ｉ		
太平洋高気圧	Taiheiyō kōkiatsu	太平洋 the Pacific Ocean, 高気圧 high pressure, 太平洋高気圧 high pressure system of the Pacific Ocean
勢い	ikioi	power
全国的に	zenkokuteki ni	nation-wide
晴天	seiten	fine weather, sunny weather
各地	kakuchi	many places, all parts
最高気温	saikō kion	最高 the highest, 気温 temperature 最高気温 the highehest temperature
記録する	kiroku suru	to record

	広島	Hiroshima	Hiroshima City
	長崎	Nagasaki	Nagasaki City
	原爆記念日	Genbaku Kinenbi	Anniversaries of the Atomic Bombings of Hiroshima and Nagasaki (→P. 54)
	終戦記念日	Shūsen Kinenbi	the Anniversary of the End of World War II (→P. 54)
	平和	heiwa	peace
	祈る	inoru	to pray
	集会	shūkai	gathering, rally
	行事	gyōji	event
	行われます	okonawaremasu	行う to hold
5	お-盆	O-bon	the Buddhist Festival of the Dead (→P. 52)
	仏教	Bukkyō	the Buddhism
	なくなった	nakunatta	なくなる to pass away
	先祖	senzo	ancestors
	霊	rei	soul
	迎え火	mukaebi	welcome fire
	たいたり	taitari	たく to light
	仏だん	butsudan	Buddhist's alter kept at each household
	そなえたり	sonaetari	そなえる to offer, to place as an offering
	準備	junbi	preparation
	盆踊り	bon odori	*bon* dance (→P. 52)
	花火大会	hanabi taikai	fireworks display
	あちらこちらで	achira kochira de	here and there, in many places
	さかんに	sakan ni	extensively
	送り火	okuribi	send-off fire (→P. 53)
	見送ります	miokurimasu	見送る to see off
	京都	Kyōto	Kyoto City
	大文字の送り火	Daimonji no okuribi	huge *Daimonji* send-off fire in Kyoto (→P. 53)
	とうろう流し	tōrō nagashi	floating paper lantern (→P.52)
10	地方	chihō	region, area
	商店	shōten	store
	お-盆休み	O-bon yasumi	*O-bon* holidays (→P. 53)
	利用して	riyō shite	利用する to make use of
	帰省したり	kisei shitari	帰省する to travel to one's hometown (→P. 53)
	空港	kūkō	airport
	お-みやげ	o-miyage	souvenir
	長距離列車	chōkyori ressha	長距離 long distance, 列車 train 長距離列車 long distance train

交通機関	kōtsū kikan	交通 transportation, 機関 system
		交通機関 transportation system
大混雑します	dai-konzatsu shimasu	大混雑する to be very congested
幹線道路	kansen dōro	幹線 major, 道路 road, high way
		幹線道路 major high way
数十キロ	sūjikkiro	tens of kilometers
列	retsu	line

15 全国高校野球選手権大会　Zenkoku Kōkōyakyū Senshuken Taikai

		全国 all-Japan, 高校 high school,
		野球 baseball, 選手権大会 tournament
		全国高校野球選手権大会 The All-Japan High
		School Baseball Tournament　　　(→P. 54)
日本全国	Nihon zenkoku	all over Japan
地区予選	chiku yosen	地区 region, 予選 tournament,
		地区予選 regional tournament
勝ち抜いた	kachi nuita	勝ち抜く to win
チーム	chiimu	team
兵庫県	Hyōgo-ken	Hyogo Prefecture
甲子園球場	Kōshien Kyūjō	Koshien Baseball Stadium
日本一	Nihon'ichi	No. 1 in Japan
競います	kisoimasu	競う to compete
各県代表	kakuken daihyō	各県 each prefecture, 代表 representative
		各県代表 representative of each prefecture
出場している	shutsujō shite iru	出場する to be in the tournament
人々	hitobito	people
自分	jibun	self
出身県	shusshinken	home/native prefecture
地元	jimoto	home, locality where one lives
応援します	ōen shimasu	応援する to cheer
20 高校野球	kōkō yakyū	The All-Japan High School Baseball
		Tournament　　　(→P. 54)
近づき	chikazuki	近づく to get close

9月

P. ℓ.				
58 1	夏休み	natsuyasumi	summer vacation	
	ほとんど	hotondo	most	
	2学期	ni-gakki	second term	
	学年	gakunen	school year	
	真ん中	man'naka	middle	
	学期	gakki	term	
	あたり	atari	あたる to fall on	
	運動会	undōkai	athletic meeting, field day	(→P. 68)
	学園祭	gakuensai	campus festival	(→P. 72)
	行事	gyōji	event	
	時期	jiki	time	
	防災の日	Bōsai no Hi	Disaster Prevention Day	(→P. 60)
	関東大震災	Kantō Daishinsai	the Great Kanto Earthquake	(→P. 60)
	惨事	sanji	disaster	
	くりかえさない	kurikaesanai	くりかえす to repeat	
5	全国	zenkoku	all over the country	
	役所	yakusho	public and municipal offices	
	地域	chiiki	community	
	避難訓練	hinan kunren	earthquake and fire drills	(→P. 60)
	行われます	okonawaremasu	行う to hold	
	台風	taifū	typhoon	(→P. 60)
	影響	eikyō	influence	
	たおれたり	taoretari	たおれる to crash	
	農作物	nōsakubutsu	crop	
	被害が出たり	higai ga detari	被害が出る to be ruined	
	洪水が起ったり	kōzui ga okottari	洪水が起る to be flooded	
	大型台風	ōgata taifū	大型 big, 台風 typhoon	
			大型台風 big typhoon	
	近づいてくる	chikazuite kuru	近づく to get close to	
	テレビ	terebi	television	
	ラジオ	rajio	radio	
	進路	shinro	course	
	風速	fūsoku	wind velocity	
	降水量	kōsuiryō	amount of rainfall	
	台風情報	taifū jōhō	typhoon information	
	放送します	hōsō shimasu	放送する to broadcast	

9月の前半	ku-gatsu no zenhan	the first half of September
太平洋高気圧	Taiheiyō kōkiatsu	太平洋 the Pacific Ocean, 高気圧 high pressure, 太平洋高気圧 high pressure system of the Pacific Ocean
残暑	zansho	late summer heat
きびしい	kibishii	strong
中旬	chūjun	the middle ten days of the month, midmonth
10 気温	kion	temperature
秋らしくなってきます	akirashiku natte kimasu	秋らしくなる Autumn is in the air.
夜長	yonaga	long night
こおろぎ	kōrogi	cricket
きりぎりす	kirigirisu	grasshopper
声	koe	chirp
虫の音	mushi no ne	music of insects
楽しんでいます	tanoshinde imasu	楽しむ to enjoy
満月	mangetsu	the full moon
中秋の名月	Chūshū no Meigetsu	beautiful moon of mid-autumn (→P. 62)
昔	mukashi	olden times, ancient time
1年中で	ichinenjū de	all the year around
お-月見	o-tsukimi	moon viewing (→P. 62)
月見だんご	tsukimi dango	dumplings offered to the moon
すすき	susuki	Japanese pampas grass
15 ぶどう	budō	grapes
くり	kuri	chestnut
季節	kisetsu	season
くだもの	kudamono	fruit
そなえて	sonaete	そなえる to offer
鑑賞する	kanshō suru	to appreciate
高層ビル	kōsō biru	highrise building
マンション	manshon	apartment (building)
日常生活	nichijō seikatsu	日常 every day, daily, 生活 life, 日常生活 daily life
敬老の日	Keirō no Hi	Respect for the Aged Day (→P. 61)
お-年寄り	o-toshiyori	elderly people
感謝する	kansha suru	to express gratitude
秋分の日	Shūbun no Hi	the Autumnnal Equinox
中心として	chūshin to shite	around
お-彼岸	o-higan	a week around the Equinox (→P. 24)

20 お-墓参り	o-hakamairi	visiting the graves of one's ancestors	(→P. 24)
しだいに	shidaini	gradually	

10月

P. ℓ. 64	衣替え	koromogae	change of dress	(→P. 40)
	制服	seifuku	uniform	
	冬服	fuyufuku	winter uniforms/clothes	
	かわります	kawarimasu	かわる to change	
	赤い羽根共同募金	Akai Hane Kyōdō Bokin	the Red Feathers Community Chest Campaign	
				(→P. 68)
	有志	yūshi	volunteer	
	募金活動	bokin katsudō	募金 fund-raising, 活動 activity	
			募金活動 fund-raising activity	
	募金箱	bokinbako	collection box	
	胸	mune	breast	
5	体育の日	Taiiku no Hi	Health-Sports Day	
	東京オリンピック	Tōkyō Orinpikku	the Tokyo Olympics	
	開会式	kaikaishiki	opening ceremony	
	記念して	kinen shite	記念する to commemorate	
	スポーツ	supōtsu	sport	
	楽しむ	tanoshimu	to enjoy	
	この日を中心に	kono hi o chūshin ni	around this day	
	幼稚園	yōchien	kindergarten	
	町内会	chōnaikai	community association	
	運動会	undōkai	athletic meeting, field day	(→P. 68)
	開きます	hirakimasu	開く to have	
	家族	kazoku	family	
	お-弁当	o-bentō	lunch box	
	参加します	sanka shimasu	参加する to join	
	下旬	gejun	the latter part of the month	
			the last ten days of the month	
	競馬	keiba	horse racing	(→P. 68)
	天皇賞レース	Ten'nōshō Rēsu	the Emperor's Cup Horse Race	
	プロ野球	puro yakyū	professional baseball	(→P. 30)
	日本シリーズ	Nihon Shiriizu	the Japan Series	
	国民体育大会	Kokumin Taiiku Taikai	Nationwide Sports Events	

10 結婚式	kekkonshiki	wedding ceremony	(→P. 66)
大安	Taian	the most lucky day (on the *Rokuyō* calendar)	
吉日	kichijitsu	lucky day	(→P. 67)
ホテル	hoteru	hotel	
結婚式場	kekkon shikijō	結婚 wedding,　式場 hall, 結婚式場 wedding hall	
神社	jinja	shrine	
教会	kyōkai	church	
つぎつぎに	tsugitsugini	one after another	
あげられます	ageraremasu	あげる to celebrate	
スタイル	sutairu	style	
宗教	shūkyō	religion	
関係ありません	kankei arimasen	関係ある to have something to do with	
式の後	shiki no ato	after the ceremony	
披露宴	hirōen	wedding reception	
行われます	okonawaremasu	行う to hold	
花よめ	hanayome	bride	
花むこ	hanamuko	bridegroom	
お-色直し	o-ironaoshi	changing costumes during a wedding reception	
年々	nen'nen	year after year	
はなやかに	hanayaka ni	elaborately	
15 おだやかな	odayaka na	calm and comfortable	
気候	kikō	weather	
さわやかな	sawayaka na	fresh	
秋晴れ	akibare	fine autumn day	
続きます	tsuzukimasu	続く to continue	
時期	jiki	time	
行楽	kōraku	outing	
シーズン	shiizun	season	
家族連れ	kazokuzure	with family	
果樹園	kajuen	orchard	
なしもぎ	nashimogi	pear-picking	
りんご狩り	ringogari	apple-picking	
楽しみます	tanoshimimasu	楽しむ to enjoy	
野山	noyama	hill and field	
木の実	konomi	nuts	
幼稚園児	yōchienji	kindergartener	

小学生	shōgakusei	schoolchildren
くりひろい	kurihiroi	chestnut-gathering
いもほり	imohori	sweet potato-digging
出かけます	dekakemasu	出かける to go out
都会	tokai	city
やおや	yaoya	greengrocer
店先	misesaki	the store front
まつたけ	matsutake	*matsutake* mushroom
なし	nashi	pear
くり	kuri	chestnut
かき	kaki	persimmon
ならび	narabi	ならぶ to be displayed
20 新米	shinmai	newly-harvested rice
出始めます	de hajimemasu	出始める to appear
さば	saba	mackerel
いわし	iwashi	sardine
さんま	sanma	saury pike

11月

P. ℓ. 70 1 だんだん	dandan	gradually
日本列島	Nihon rettō	Japanese Archipelago
各地	kakuchi	many places, all parts
紅葉	kōyō	autumn foliage
もみじ	momiji	maple
いちょう	ichō	ginkgo tree
色づき始める	irozuki hajimeru	to begin to change colors
人々	hitobito	people
名所	meisho	famous spot, noted place
出かけます	dekakemasu	出かける to go out
もみじ狩り	momijigari	autumn foliage viewing
季節	kisetsu	season
楽しみ	tanoshimi	pleasure
文化の日	Bunka no Hi	Culture Day
祝日	shukujitsu	national holiday
芸術	geijutsu	art
学術	gakujutsu	scholarship

すぐれた	sugureta	outstanding	
5 皇居	kōkyo	the Imperial Palace	
文化勲章	Bunka Kunshō	the Order of Culture	(→P. 72)
おくられます	okuraremasu	おくる to give, to award, to present	
展覧会	tenrankai	exhibition	
音楽会	ongakukai	concert	
芸術祭	geijutsusai	art festival	
開かれ	hirakare	開く to have	
学芸会	gakugeikai	performing arts festival	
文化祭	bunkasai	culture fair	(→P. 72)
行われます	okonawaremasu	行う to hold	
りっぱな	rippa na	grand	
美術館	bijutsukan	art museum	
ホール	hōru	(concert) hall	
文化活動	bunka katsudō	文化 culture, 活動 activity	
		文化活動 culture activity	
さかんになってきました	sakan ni natte kimashita	さかんになる to become popular	
七五三	Shichi-go-san	*Shichi-go-san* Celebration	(→P. 73)
地方	chihō	locality	
10 晴れ着	haregi	formal clothes	
神社	jinja	shrine	
お参り	omairi	to pay a visit to a temple or a shrine	
千歳飴	chitoseame	special candy for *Shichi-go-san* Celebration	
			(→P. 73)
記念写真	kinen shashin	記念 commemoration, 写真 photograph	
		記念写真 commemorative photograph	
家族	kazoku	family	
そろって	sorotte	together	
レストラン	resutoran	restaurant	
ごちそう	gochisō	special feast	
成長	seichō	growth	
祝います	iwaimasu	祝う to celebrate	
勤労感謝の日	Kinrō Kansha no Hi	Labor Thanksgiving Day	
下町	shitamachi	downtown	
酉の市	Tori no Ichi	*Tori no Ichi* Festival	(→P. 72)
くまで	kumade	rake	
15 商売繁盛	shōbai hanjō	商売 business, 繁盛 thriving	
		商売繁盛 thriving business	

願う	negau	to wish for
まつり	matsuri	festival
近づき	chikazuki	近づく to get close to
年の暮	toshi no kure	the end of the year
北風	kitakaze	north wind
吹き始め	fuki hajime	吹き始める to begin to blow
北海道	Hokkaidō	Hokkaido
東北	Tōhoku	Tohoku area
北陸地方	Hokuriku chihō	Hokuriku area
本格的な	honkakuteki na	full-scale
迎えます	mukaemasu	迎える to brace for
関東地方	Kantō chihō	Kanto area
家庭	katei	household
かたずけておいた	katazukete oita	かたずける to store
ストーブ	sutōbu	heater
こたつ	kotatsu	traditional Japanese heating equipment
暖房器具	danbō kigu	暖房 heating, 器具 equipment
		暖房器具 heating equipment
したく	shitaku	preparation

12月

P.76 ℓ. しめくくり	shimekukuri	final settlement	
師走	Shiwasu	another old name for December	(→P. 78)
上旬	jōjun	the first ten days of the month	
		the first part of the month	
ボーナス	bōnasu	bonus	(→P. 41)
お-中元	o-chūgen	midsummer gift	(→P. 47)
日頃	higoro	usually	
お-世話になった	o-sewa ni natta	世話になる to be taken care of,	
		to be shown kindness	
感謝をこめて	kansha o komete	感謝をこめる to express grateful feelings	
お-歳暮	o-seibo	year-end present	
クリスマス	Kurisumasu	Christmas	
お-正月	o-shōgatsu	the New Year holiday period	
買い物客	kaimonokyaku	shopper	
デパート	depāto	department store	

商店街	shōtengai	shopping street/area
にぎわいます	nigiwaimasu	にぎわう to be crowded
5 年賀特別郵便取扱	nenga tokubetsu	special acceptance of New Year's cards
	yūbin toriatsukai	in advance for deliveries on New Year's Day
開始されます	kaishi saremasu	開始する to begin
郵便局	yūbinkyoku	post office
元日	ganjitsu	New Year's Day
年賀状	nengajō	New Year's greeting card (→P. 79)
配達する	haitatsu suru	to deliver
アルバイト	arubaito	part timer, extra staff
やとって	yatotte	やとう to employ, to hire
準備します	junbi shimasu	準備する to prepare
冬至	Tōji	Winter Solstice
かぼちゃ	kabocha	pumpkin
ゆず湯	yuzuyu	bath with *yuzu* (a kind of Japanese variety of citrus fruit)
かぜ	kaze	cold, influenza
予防し	yobō shi	予防する to prevent
すごせる	sugoseru	すごす to pass
冬休み	fuyuyasumi	winter vacation
10 天皇誕生日	Ten'nō Tanjōbi	the Birthday of Emperor Akihito
祝日	shukujitsu	national holiday
人々	hitobito	people
宗教	shūkyō	religion
関係なく	kankei naku	regardless of
楽しみます	tanoshimimasu	楽しむ to enjoy
町	machi	town
クリスマスツリー	Kurisumasu tsurii	Christmas tree
かざられ	kazarare	かざる to decorate
ジングルベル	Jinguru Beru	Jingle Bells
メロディー	merodii	melody
流れて	nagarete	流れる to float
おたがいに	otagaini	each other
プレゼント	purezento	present
交換したり	kōkan shitari	交換する to exchange
クリスマスケーキ	Kurisumasu kēki	Christmas cake
にぎやかに	nigiyaka ni	merrily
時期	jiki	time

忘年会	bōnenkai	year-end party	(→P. 78)
さかんに	sakan ni	frequently	
開かれます	hirakaremasu	開く to have, to hold	
15 官公庁	kankōchō	goverment and municipal offices	
御用納め	goyō osame	the last work day for goverment and municipal offices	
役所	yakusho	goverment and municipal offices (approximately same as *kankōchō*)	
年末年始	nenmatsu nenshi	年末 year-end　　年始 New Year 年末年始 year-end and New Year	
休暇	kyūka	holidays	
空港	kūkō	airport	
ふるさと	furusato	home town	
海外旅行	kaigai ryokō	海外 overseas,　　旅行 travel 海外旅行 overseas travel	(→P. 36)
スキー場	sukiijō	ski area	
こみあいます	komiaimasu	こみあう to be crowded	
正月かざり	shōgatsu kazari	New Year's decorations	(→P. 79)
食品売り場	shokuhin uriba	食品 food,　　売り場 section, 食品売り場 food section	
正月料理	shōgatsu ryōri	New Year's special food	(→P. 10)
20 いっぱいになります	ippai ni narimasu	いっぱいになる to be packed	
各家庭	kaku katei	each household	
大掃除	ō-sōji	general house cleaning	(→P. 80)
迎える	mukaeru	迎える to greet	
準備	junbi	preparation	
大晦日	ōmisoka	New Year's Eve	(→P. 80)
年越しそば	toshikoshi soba	buckwheat noodles eaten on New Year's Eve	(→P. 80)
テレビ	terebi	television	
ラジオ	rajio	radio	
中継される	chūkei sareru	中継する to broadcast	
全国	zenkoku	whole country	
寺院	jiin	temple	
除夜の鐘	Joya no Kane	New Year's Eve Bells	(→P. 80)

国際日本語研究所

編集スタッフ

臼 田 敦 子（USUDA, Atsuko）

宇佐美 章子（USAMI, Ayako）

佐藤 由紀子（SATO, Yukiko）

花 田 昌 子（HANADA, Masako）

股 野 儷 子（MATANO, Reiko）

翻訳協力

メリー・ギャンズ（Mary GANZ）

写真提供

芦田 直大

株式会社 虎屋

鳥取県東京物産観光センター

狭山市観光協会

井関農機株式会社

株式会社 自立学習社

たのしく読める

日本のくらし12ヵ月
Moons, Months and Seasons

1992年3月31日　初版発行	定価 1,850円
1992年6月30日　第2版発行	（本体 1,796円）

編　者　　国際日本語研究所

発行者　　竹　内　美佐恵

発行所　　株式会社　杏　文　堂
　　　　　〒101 東京都千代田区猿楽町2-8-16
　　　　　電　話 03-3293-1377

Ⓒ1992 Printed in Japan.　　　印刷：大熊整美堂　　製本：㈲精光堂
　　　　　　　　　　　　　　　ISBN4-905737-12-5 C0081

杏文堂の 日本語教材

FOR FUN Series

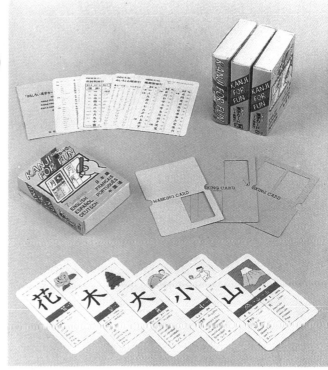

おもしろい漢字カード
KANJI FOR FUN (80 cards)
各1240円

(1) 学年別配当漢字 76字(1年)
(2) 学年別配当漢字145字(2年)
(3)

〈各巻 B7判ケース入り（80枚セット）〉
〈日・英・仏・スペイン・ポルトガル・独・中国語の7ヶ国語解説書付〉

　文部省学年別配当に準拠した最も基本的な漢字をカード化したものです。
　カードのイモテには、漢字本体と漢字の形をわかりやすく示したカラーイラストと象形文字、その漢字の最も代表的な音読み、訓読みを使った単語が示してあります（7ヵ国語付）。カードのウラには白ヌキの漢字の中にその書き順を示す矢印と番号が示されています。カラフルなイラストや、よく用いられる単語を通して、漢字の読み方や正しい書き順が楽しく覚えられるカードです。

Basic KANJI for reading and stroke recognition are taught with frequently used words and colorful illustrations. (7 languages: Japanese, English, French, Spanish, Portuguese, German, Chinese)

おもしろいひらがな
HIRAGANA FOR FUN
おもしろいカタカナ
KATAKANA FOR FUN

〈B5判　64頁 ワークブック〉　各960円

　絵から学べる楽しいひらがな・カタカナ入門書。絵と音の組み合わせによって、短期間にマスターできる楽しい独習書。

Beginner's Hiragana/Katakana Workbook.
Pictures do the teaching.

おもしろいあいさつカード
DAILY EXPRESSIONS IN JAPANESE
(48 cards)　　3090円
〈B5判 48枚 パッケージ入り〉
〈6ヵ国語訳インデックスカード付〉

　クリちゃんの楽しいイラストとともに、日本語のあいさつ、きまり文句が自然に覚えられる楽しいフラッシュカード

Conversational Japanese phrases and expressions are taught through pictures.

おもしろいカタカナ
KATAKANA FOR FUN (48 cards)
— Flash Cards —

〈B5判 カラー48枚 パッケージ入り〉3914円

　カラフルなイラストと国名、地名の文字を組み合わせて覚える楽しいカタカナカード。（6ヵ国語訳インデックスカード付）日本語の学習と同時に、世界への広い視野と大きな心をはぐくむ、楽しい教室用教材

48 colorful Katakana is introduced in combination with 45 country and city names.

美しい日本と子どもの くらし　I KNOW JAPAN (56 pages)

〈B5判 56頁 テキストブック〉　875円

　日本の子どもたちの身近な風俗・習慣を中心に今日の日本の姿を写真によって紹介するテキストブック。日本の文化を知るための社会科教材として生きた日本語の学習に最適。

Children's treasury about Japan, it introduces the country, the culture, customs and interesting sights.